READINGS ON

PRIDE AND PREJUDICE

Other titles in the Greenhaven Press Literary Companion Series:

American Authors

Maya Angelou
Stephen Crane
Emily Dickinson
William Faulkner
F. Scott Fitzgerald
Nathaniel Hawthorne
Ernest Hemingway
Herman Melville
Arthur Miller
Eugene O'Neill
Edgar Allan Poe
John Steinbeck
Mark Twain
Thornton Wilder

American Literature

The Adventures of
  Huckleberry Finn
The Adventures of Tom
  Sawyer
The Catcher in the Rye
The Crucible
Death of a Salesman
The Glass Menagerie
The Grapes of Wrath
The Great Gatsby
Of Mice and Men
The Old Man and the Sea
The Pearl
The Scarlet Letter
A Separate Peace

British Authors

Jane Austen
Joseph Conrad
Charles Dickens

British Literature

Animal Farm
The Canterbury Tales
Great Expectations
Hamlet
Julius Caesar
Lord of the Flies
Macbeth
Romeo and Juliet
Shakespeare: The Comedies
Shakespeare: The Histories
Shakespeare: The Sonnets
Shakespeare: The Tragedies
A Tale of Two Cities
Wuthering Heights

World Authors

Fyodor Dostoyevsky
Homer
Sophocles

World Literature

A Doll's House
All Quiet on the Western
  Front
The Diary of a Young Girl

THE GREENHAVEN PRESS
Literary Companion
TO BRITISH LITERATURE

READINGS ON

PRIDE AND PREJUDICE

Clarice Swisher, *Book Editor*

David L. Bender, *Publisher*
Bruno Leone, *Executive Editor*
Bonnie Szumski, *Series Editor*

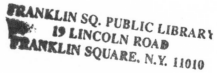
Greenhaven Press, Inc., San Diego, CA

Every effort has been made to trace the owners of copy-
righted material. The articles in this volume may have
been edited for content, length, and/or reading level. The
titles have been changed to enhance the editorial purpose.
Those interested in locating the original source will find
the complete citation on the first page of each article.

Library of Congress Cataloging-in-Publication Data

Readings on Pride and prejudice / Clarice Swisher, book
    editor.
        p.   cm. — (The Greenhaven Press literary
    companion to British literature)
        Includes bibliographical references (p.   ) and index.
    ISBN 1-56510-861-2 (lib. bdg. : alk. paper). —
    ISBN 1-56510-860-4 (pbk. : alk. paper)
        1. Austen, Jane, 1775–1817. Pride and prejudice.
    I. Swisher, Clarice, 1933–   . II. Series.
    PR4034.P73R43   1999
    823'.7—dc21   98-8437
                                                  CIP

Copyright ©1999 by Greenhaven Press, Inc.
PO Box 289009
San Diego, CA 92198-9009
Printed in the U.S.A.

66I must confess that I think her [Elizabeth] as delightful a creature as ever appeared in print. 99

CONTENTS

they have mortified, or humiliated, each other. Elizabeth's rejection of Darcy's first proposal and his followup letter set the process in motion, altering character to make love possible.

Chapter 5: Irony and Wit

FOREWORD

*"'Tis the good reader that
makes the good book."*

Ralph Waldo Emerson

The story's bare facts are simple: The captain, an old and
scarred seafarer, walks with a peg leg made of whale ivory.
He relentlessly drives his crew to hunt the world's oceans for
the great white whale that crippled him. After a long search,
the ship encounters the whale and a fierce battle ensues. Finally the captain drives his harpoon into the whale, but the
harpoon line catches the captain about the neck and drags
him to his death.

A simple story, a straightforward plot—yet, since the 1851
publication of Herman Melville's *Moby-Dick*, readers and
critics have found many meanings in the struggle between
Captain Ahab and the whale. To some, the novel is a cau-
tionary tale that depicts how Ahab's obsession with revenge
leads to his insanity and death. Others believe that the whale
represents the unknowable secrets of the universe and that
Ahab is a tragic hero who dares to challenge fate by attempt-
ing to discover this knowledge. Perhaps Melville intended
Ahab as a criticism of Americans' tendency to become involved in well-intentioned but irrational causes. Or did
Melville model Ahab after himself, letting his fictional character express his anger at what he perceived as a cruel and
distant god?

Although literary critics disagree over the meaning of
Moby-Dick, readers do not need to choose one particular interpretation in order to gain an understanding of Melville's

novel. Instead, by examining various analyses, they can gain numerous insights into the issues that lie under the surface of the basic plot. Studying the writings of literary critics can also aid readers in making their own assessments of *Moby-Dick* and other literary works and in developing analytical thinking skills.

The Greenhaven Literary Companion Series was created with these goals in mind. Designed for young adults, this unique anthology series provides an engaging and comprehensive introduction to literary analysis and criticism. The essays included in the Literary Companion Series are chosen for their accessibility to a young adult audience and are expertly edited in consideration of both the reading and comprehension levels of this audience. In addition, each essay is introduced by a concise summation that presents the contributing writer's main themes and insights. Every anthology in the Literary Companion Series contains a varied selection of critical essays that cover a wide time span and express diverse views. Wherever possible, primary sources are represented through excerpts from authors' notebooks, letters, and journals and through contemporary criticism.

Each title in the Literary Companion Series pays careful consideration to the historical context of the particular author or literary work. In-depth biographies and detailed chronologies reveal important aspects of authors' lives and emphasize the historical events and social milieu that influenced their writings. To facilitate further research, every anthology includes primary and secondary source bibliographies of articles and/or books selected for their suitability for young adults. These engaging features make the Greenhaven Literary Companion series ideal for introducing students to literary analysis in the classroom or as a library resource for young adults researching the world's great authors and literature.

Exceptional in its focus on young adults, the Greenhaven Literary Companion Series strives to present literary criticism in a compelling and accessible format. Every title in the series is intended to spark readers' interest in leading American and world authors, to help them broaden their understanding of literature, and to encourage them to formulate their own analyses of the literary works that they read. It is the editors' hope that young adult readers will find these anthologies to be true companions in their study of literature.

INTRODUCTION

Readings on Pride and Prejudice reflects Jane Austen's description of her own work; in a letter to her brother Edward, she identified it as "the little bit (two inches wide) of ivory on which I work with so fine a brush." Critics of *Pride and Prejudice* rework a limited number of topics relevant to the novel—the theme of pride and prejudice, irony, dialogue, foolish and intelligent characters—and, like Austen, they work with a fine brush. Though the range is narrow, each critic offers a distinguishing view or angle, subtly different from any other. Taken together, the essays in this companion present a picture of *Pride and Prejudice* painted in fine brush strokes.

Established Austen critics from the 1950s, such as Dorothy Van Ghent, Andrew Wright, Marvin Mudrick, and Rueben Brower, are represented in this book; a majority of contributors, however, have published their work in the last two decades, during a resurgence of interest in Austen perhaps prompted by the bicentennial of her birth in 1775.

Readings on Pride and Prejudice includes many special features that make research and literary criticism accessible and understandable. An annotated table of contents lets readers quickly preview the contents of individual essays. A chronology features a list of significant events in Austen's life placed in a broader historical context. The bibliography provides sources that include books on Austen's time and additional critical sources suitable for further research. In addition, names and addresses of two Austen societies make additional information available.

Each essay has aids for clear understanding. The introductions explain main points, which are then identified by subheads within the essays. Footnotes identify uncommon references and define unfamiliar words. Inserts, many taken from the novel, illustrate points made in the essays. Together these aids make the Greenhaven Press Literary Companion Series an indispensable research tool.

JANE AUSTEN: A BIOGRAPHY

Jane Austen, considered England's first great woman novelist, was born in the village of Steventon, Hampshire, on December 16, 1775, and lived her whole life within a small area in southwestern England. Austen, who lived during the Napoleonic Wars, the revolutions in America and France, and the coming Industrial Revolution, kept abreast of issues in the world at large, but she focused her writing on the social life of England's middle and upper classes living in small villages and in rural areas. Determined to write only about what she knew, she observed behavior with a perceptive eye and portrayed human traits realistically. She is the author of six major novels, three written in her early twenties and the other three in her late thirties. Her letters to her sister Cassandra and to other family members have also been published, and remain a valuable resource for biographers, scholars, and critics.

Austen grew up in England during the late eighteenth century in a society with strict social classes and clearly defined roles. At the top of the social order was the aristocracy, men and women with titles and enough inherited wealth to live comfortably without working. Next was the middle class, called the gentry, composed of wealthy landowners, prosperous businessmen, military officers, and professional people. Below the gentry were paid laborers, ordinary soldiers and sailors, and subsistence farmers. At the bottom of the social order were the servants, who lived and worked on the estates of the upper classes for little pay. While the women in the lower classes worked hard at physical tasks to help supply food, clothing, and shelter for their families, women in the upper classes were expected to follow strict rules of decorum that governed their conversation in social situations and their relations with men. Women were trained in music, drawing, and the domestic arts of embroidery and sewing. They could not attend universities and were expected to have no opinions about intellectual matters or political issues. Three choices were available to them: They could marry, preferably landing a prosperous husband; they could spend their lives as spinsters living in their parents' or other relatives' homes; or they could become governesses or teachers and be sustained in the homes of the wealthy.

AUSTEN'S FAMILY

Jane Austen's ancestors on her father's side were gentry from near Canterbury in Kent in southeastern England. Dating back to the Middle Ages, her ancestors raised sheep and manufactured clothing; eventually, one branch of the family carried on the business and became very wealthy, and the other branch entered professions. Jane's father, George Austen, the son of a surgeon, was orphaned before he was nine and left penniless; however, his wealthy uncle, Francis Austen, a lawyer, raised him as one of his own children. He sent George to St. John's College at Oxford, where he became a distinguished scholar and fellow, or teacher. An unusually good-looking man, he was known at the university as "the handsome proctor." After teaching for a time, he took Holy Orders, making him eligible to be a rector in the Anglican Church. It was the custom for wealthy persons to act as patrons and pay the living expenses of ministers. George's distant cousin, Thomas Knight, purchased a position for George Austen at the rectory in Steventon, and his uncle Francis purchased the rectory for him at Deane, the neighboring church.

Jane Austen's ancestors on her mother's side, dating back to the Norman Conquest of England in 1066, settled in the west near Windsor. Jane's mother, Cassandra Leigh, descended from a distinguished line including Sir Thomas Leigh, lord mayor of London, and Oxford scholars, Sir Thomas White, founder of St. John's College; Theophilus Leigh, a well-known wit of the time and master of Balliol College; and Thomas Leigh, her father, fellow at All Soul's College. Cassandra Leigh met the handsome George Austen at the university's social gatherings in Oxford. Cassandra's family was upper gentry and George's family lower gentry, but the couple fell in love and were married at Walcot Church in the city of Bath on August 26, 1764. They settled first at Deane and shortly after at Steventon.

Jane was the seventh of eight children born to George and Cassandra Austen between 1765 and 1779. James, the oldest, followed in his father's footsteps and became rector of Steventon when his father retired. Nothing is known about

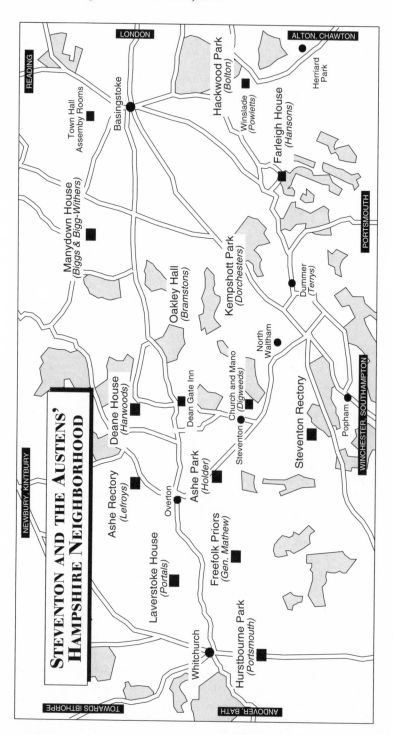

George, who had physical and mental disorders, except that he lived in the area near Steventon. Third son Edward, adopted by Thomas Knight, a wealthy, childless distant relative, grew up in Kent in the Knight household and took the Knight name in order to inherit the family estate. Jane's favorite brother Henry, especially charming and good looking, served as a colonel in the Oxfordshire Militia before becoming a London banker and eventually a clergyman. Cassandra, two years older than Jane, was Jane's confidante and closest companion throughout her life. Francis, called Frank, entered the navy at twelve, reached the rank of admiral, and was knighted for his bravery and service in battle. Like Frank, Charles, the youngest Austen child, had a distinguished navy career. The Austens were devoted parents who nurtured bright, spirited children. In *A Memory of Jane Austen*, Jane's nephew James E. Austen-Leigh describes the congeniality and closeness of the Austen family:

> This was the small circle. . . . There was so much that was agreeable and attractive in this family party that its members may be excused if they were inclined to live somewhat too exclusively within it. They might see in each other much to love and esteem, and something to admire. The family talk had abundance of spirit and vivacity, and was never troubled by disagreements even in little matters, for it was not their habit to dispute or argue with each other; above all, there was strong family affection and firm union, never to be broken but by death.

George Austen lived the life of a gentleman and scholar at Steventon and provided well for his family. Besides his work as the clergyman of two churches, he supplemented his income by farming the land around the rectory and by tutoring not only his own sons, but also boys from other families who paid for his services as teacher. With sufficient income to build additions to the house and improve the grounds, he made their home superior to other country parsonages, and with his status and money, he provided what his family needed to enjoy the social life of an English country gentleman. The Austens had horses and carriages, which symbolized wealth. The family visited relatives and friends and hosted return visits in the style of the aristocracy and gentry, whose outlook, manners, and language were alike. In *A Portrait of Jane Austen*, biographer and critic David Cecil clarifies a few differences between the two ruling classes:

> The Steventon district had its great nobles . . . who were on sufficiently equal terms with their humbler gentry neighbours to invite them to a big ball or a garden fete once or twice in the

year. But they did not expect to be invited back, and at other times they did not mix with them. . . . Well-connected, well-mannered and traditionally Tory, the Austens were qualified in every respect to be welcomed into the inner circle of this society; and all the more because Thomas Knight, chief landowner of the district, lived in Kent, leaving George Austen as his representative to be consulted and deferred to as an acting squire.

Jane grew up in a comfortable cultural and family environment which molded her attitudes in childhood and influenced her thoughts in adulthood.

AUSTEN'S EDUCATION AND EARLY WRITING

The values and status of Jane's family definitely affected her education. Her mother oversaw the training in needlework, music, and dancing. In 1782, when Cassandra was eight, the family arranged to send her to Mrs. Cawley's school in Oxford, and because Jane so closely identified with her sister, they sent her too, even though she was only six. Mrs. Austen described Jane's attachment to her sister by saying, "If Cassandra were going to have her head cut off, Jane would insist on sharing her fate." After one year, Mrs. Cawley moved her school to Southampton, but an epidemic of a disease similar to typhus called putrid throat broke out, and the girls returned home. The family sent them to the Abbey School in Reading, a loosely run school with few lessons and much play. Jane attended the Abbey School until she was eleven when she returned home to be taught by her father.

Jane acquired her education in a variety of ways. In addition to her father's lessons, Jane learned French and some Italian and studied history. She read widely from the numerous books in her father's library. George Austen had an extensive library, which included all of Shakespeare's plays and the English novels of Henry Fielding, George Smollett, and Oliver Goldsmith. His library also included contemporary popular stories; for example, *Evelina* and *Cecilia,* written by Fanny Burney, the originator of the novel of home life. Moreover, Mr. Austen read to his family regularly in the evening, and the children habitually read aloud to each other. Jane was much better educated than most girls in the late eighteenth century as critic and biographer John Halperin comments in *The Life of Jane Austen:*

> While her education was somewhat haphazard, it was a liberal one. . . . She was taught to question rather than to accept blindly; and the satirical vein very early became a favourite

with her, not least because she could be certain of addressing an audience—the family—familiar with the objects of her mirth and sympathetic to her irreverent treatment of them.

Jane began writing when she was ten or eleven years old. Her copybooks containing tales she composed as a young girl have survived. Many stories are flimsy and nonsensical, but they are all written with high spirit. She also composed plays for family parties and usually preceded them with a grandiloquent dedication, such as the one for "The Mystery. An Unfinished Comedy": "*To the Rev. George Austen.* Sir,—I humbly solicit your patronage to the following Comedy, which, though an unfinished one, is, I flatter myself, as complete a *Mystery* as any of its kind. I am, Sir, Your most humble Servant, The Author." The copybooks also record a history that Jane wrote and Cassandra illustrated. In *Jane Austen,* biographer Victor Lucas calls it

> a delightful spoof on that kind of history book which is concerned less with the facts of history than with an historian's prejudice for or against historical characters. She called it *The History of England by a Partial Prejudiced and Ignorant Historian.* It begins "Henry the 4th ascended the throne of England, much to his own satisfaction, in the year 1399." Already she is doing what she will do many times in her books—giving us, in an economical phrase, and with a twinkle of humour, an insight into the character of the person she is describing.

Cassandra depicted King Henry VIII wearing a red nightcap, appropriate, the girls concluded, for a king who had no fewer than six wedding nights.

Critics refer to Austen's childhood works as "The Juvenalia," ninety thousand words written between 1787 and 1795, including short tales, sketches, fictional letters, scraps of epistolary novels, bits of plays, and the English history. At sixteen, Jane copied all of her early works into three notebooks, entitled *Volume the First, Volume the Second, and Volume the Third.* Halperin observes: "As an adolescent she already viewed popular and sentimental fiction with the critical eye of a satirist; her early works ridicule the sentimental excesses and sensational unrealities of current popular fiction."

AUSTEN'S SOCIAL LIFE

Jane was actively involved in the family's social life. Though the Austens' favorite society was their own immediate family, many aunts, uncles, and cousins visited from Bath or Kent for a week or more. The Austens met regularly with local families to exchange morning visits, dinners, and evenings of card playing and games. They and their neighbors particularly enjoyed putting on amateur theatricals at Christmas and during the summer when the young people were home from school. Young Jane wrote prologues for the plays and helped with production while the older siblings and neighbors took the acting parts. They rehearsed such well-known comedies as Richard Sheridan's *The Rivals*, as well as less well known plays like *High Life Above Stairs, High Life Below Stairs, The Wonder: A Woman Keeps a Secret*, and *The Chances*, performing in the Austens' barn in the summer and in the dining room in the winter. These amateur theatricals were common pastimes between 1784 and 1790; Jane would draw on these experiences when writing the theatricals in *Mansfield Park*.

Much of the Steventon social activity revolved around public and private balls. Jane was an excellent dancer and often attended formal balls held in the Town Hall in Basingstoke, a nearby village. Besides its function as an important site of amusement, the ballroom served as a meeting place for young people in search of future husbands or wives. Unmarried girls attended formal balls in the company of chaperones, often their older married sisters. A master of ceremonies made the introductions and then opened the ball by partnering one of the young ladies in the first dance. To the music of a harpsichord, gentlemen and ladies, holding hands at arm's length, danced the stately minuet and quadrille. The polite society in which Jane lived considered the waltz scandalous because, as Lucas explains, "in this daring innovation from Germany they [the lady and gentleman] embraced each other, quite close, their arms around each other's waists, looking into each other's eyes, and did not let go until the music stopped." At informal dances held in homes, often at the home of Jane's neighbor and friend Mrs. Anne Lefroy, the fiddle provided music for lively country dances in which everyone participated. Young girls dancing to harpsichords or fiddles had but few years to find a husband before they were considered too old to be attractive, suitable wives.

From Cassandra's portraits and relatives' accounts, Jane Austen was considered by most an attractive young woman. In *Jane Austen and Steventon*, niece Emma Austen-Leigh reports that the earliest recorded description of Jane comes from her cousin, Philadelphia Walter, who in 1788 praised Cassandra's looks but said that Jane was "not at all pretty and very prim, unlike a girl of twelve," but Mrs. Lefroy's visiting brother said that when he knew Jane at that age, "my eyes told me she was fair and handsome, slight and elegant, but with cheeks a little too full." Her nephew, J. E. Austen-Leigh gives a detailed description in *A Memoir of Jane Austen:*

> In person she was very attractive; her figure was rather tall and slender, her step light and firm, and her whole appearance expressive of health and animation. In complexion she was a clear brunette with a rich colour; she had full round cheeks, with mouth and nose small and well formed, bright hazel eyes, and brown hair forming natural curls close round her face. If not so regularly handsome as her sister, yet her countenance had a peculiar charm of its own to the eyes of most beholders.

Jane grew out of her twelve-year-old primness and improved in appearance; in 1791 another cousin, Eliza, spoke of both Cassandra and Jane as "perfect beauties" who were gaining "hearts by the dozens," and they were "two of the prettiest girls in England."

AUSTEN AS A YOUNG WOMAN

By the time Jane reached adolescence, her comfortable, secure world had begun to expand and change. Until she was twelve, Jane had never traveled farther than to Bath, about a hundred miles away, to visit her mother's brother's family, the Leigh-Perrots. At twelve, she and Cassandra traveled by carriage with their parents to Kent, stopping in London on the way, a trip requiring several days. This was the first of many trips she made to London and Kent. During her teen years, her immediate family shrank when two of her brothers went away to college at Oxford and two joined the navy. But her extended family grew as cousins and her older brothers married and had children. Births and deaths followed one another: Her cousin Eliza, educated in France, had married a French aristocrat, the Comte de Feuillide, who became embroiled in the politics of the French Revolution and was executed by guillotine early in 1774. The following year Anne, wife of her brother James, died, leaving a two-year-old daughter, Anna, to be raised at Steventon by her grandparents and aunts.

During the 1790s, new developments affected Cassandra's and Jane's personal lives. Cassandra fell in love with Thomas Fowle, a former pupil of her father who had gone on to the university and become a clergyman. The couple were engaged in 1795, but because his rectory living was insufficient to support a family, he went to the West Indies as a chaplain to earn and save money. While in Santo Domingo he got yellow fever and died in 1797, leaving his £1000 earnings to his betrothed. Cassandra was distraught and lived in isolation for two years, during which time Jane, as her close companion, suffered with her. Cassandra never married; indeed there are no indications that she ever considered marriage again.

Jane also had a romantic interest, a flirtation with Tom Lefroy, an Irish nephew visiting the Lefroy rectory at Ashe only a few miles from Steventon. Jane's letters to Cassandra from 1796 leave it unclear if this was a mere flirtation or a serious relationship. In one letter, Jane says, "I am almost afraid to tell you how my Irish friend and I behaved. Imagine to yourself everything most profligate and shocking in the way of dancing and sitting down together. . . . He is a very gentlemanlike, good-looking, pleasant young man, I assure you." In another letter, she says she is giving up all of her other admirers "as I mean to confine myself in the future to Mr. Tom Lefroy, for whom I do not care sixpence." In another letter, she says, "I am to flirt my last with Tom Lefroy, and when you receive this it will be over. My tears flow as I write at the melancholy idea." Both Cassandra and Mrs. Lefroy were concerned that the relationship was serious and warned Jane that Tom was too young and too poor to marry. The Lefroys sent him home to Ireland, and within a year he was engaged to a woman with a large fortune.

AUSTEN'S FIRST NOVELS

The years 1796 through 1799 were significant in Jane Austen's career as a writer. By 1796, she had written part of an epistolary novel, which she called *Elinor and Marianne.* Setting it aside in October, she began a conventional novel called *First Impressions* and completed it in August 1797; the novel was later retitled *Pride and Prejudice.* By November 1797, she was busy recasting the correspondence of *Elinor and Marianne* as a narrative; she retitled it *Sense and Sensibility.* That same November saw her first attempt to find a publisher for *First Impressions.* Austen's father sent the following letter to Cadell, a London publisher:

> Sir,—I have in my possession a manuscript novel, comprising 3 vols., about the length of Miss Burney's "Evelina." As I am well aware of what consequence it is that a work of this sort shd make its first appearance under a respectable name, I apply to you. I shall be much obliged, therefore, if you will in-

form me whether you choose to be concerned in it, what will
be the expense of publishing it at the author's risk, and what
you will venture to advance for the property of it, if on perusal
it is approved of. Should you give any encouragement, I will
send you the work.

> I am, sir, your humble servant,
> George Austen.
> Steventon, near Overton, Hants,
> 1st Nov., 1797.

Cadell rejected the manuscript, and it was left to George to so
inform his daughter. In *The Story of Jane Austen's Life*, Oscar
Fay Adams comments on the difficulty for the father: "For
knowing as we do how closely the welfare of any particular
Austen was interwoven with that of all, we may be very sure
that here was a painful task for the affectionate father, so
proud of his daughter's dawning talent."

The rejection disappointed Jane but did not dampen her
desire for writing. She finished the new version of *Sense and
Sensibility* in early 1798 and immediately began another
novel, which she finished within a year. Her third novel, *Susan*, later retitled *Northanger Abbey*, differs from the first two.
Instead of being set in a village, it is set in the city of Bath and
in a remote country house. Almost entirely a satire on the romantic novels of the time, it has a heroine with whom the author has little sympathy, unlike the heroines of the first two
novels, whom Austen clearly likes. In *Susan*, the hero, Henry
Tilney, more closely represents Austen's ironic viewpoint
and has engaging traits similar to those of heroines Elinor
and Elizabeth. In the spring of 1803, Austen revised the manuscript and sold it to the publisher Crosby for £10. Though
Crosby advertised the book as "*Susan:* a Novel in 2 Volumes,"
he never published it. In 1809, he agreed to sell the manuscript back to the author for the same amount he paid for it,
but Jane could not produce the £10.

Austen's letters to her sister, Cassandra, date from 1796.
Whenever one of the girls traveled, the sisters exchanged letters. Cassandra saved many but not all of Jane's letters to her,
but destroyed all of the letters she wrote to Jane. The bulk of
Jane's remaining letters to Cassandra contain information
and impressions that typically interest single, young sisters,
sharing their daily activities and those of their family. The
most complete edition of Austen's letters, including numerous letters to other relatives, was published in two volumes
in 1932 by R. W. Chapman. Entitled *Jane Austen's Letters to
Her Sister Cassandra and Others*, the collection has been an

important source for biographers and critics searching both to define Jane Austen as a person and to interpret her novels.

AUSTEN'S PERSONALITY

Given the existence of Austen's prolific correspondence, the biographical memoir written by her nephew J.E. Austen-Leigh just over fifty years after Austen's death, and numerous diary entries relatives wrote about Jane, biographers, it seems, should find Austen's personality and character apparent and indisputable, but that is not the case. Scholars and biographers have trouble reconciling the relatives' portrayal of Jane as a model of sweetness with rather nasty lines from her letters and books that sarcastically skewer others. Some scholars argue that her satiric remarks reflect a detached and ironic style Austen cultivated for the sake of humor. Others argue that beneath the author's sweet, polite surface lurks a streak of bitterness and anger.

Austen is fondly remembered in J.E. Austen-Leigh's *Memoir*. Nieces and nephews recalling their aunt after her death particularly note her popularity with children. One remembers "her great sweetness of manner. She seemed to love you, and you loved her in return." Another remembers her aunt's helpfulness. "She would furnish us with what we wanted from her wardrobe; and she would be the entertaining visitor in our make-believe house." Yet another niece recalls her "being so playful, and her long circumstantial stories so delightful." A nephew remembers her as a community member. After recalling her love for children, he says

> but her friends of all ages felt her enlivening influence. Her unusually quick sense of the ridiculous led her to play with all the common-places of everyday life, whether as regarded persons or things; but she never played with its serious duties or responsibilities, nor did she ever turn individuals into ridicule. With all her neighbours in the village she was on friendly, though not on intimate, terms. She took a kindly interest in all their proceedings, and liked to hear about them.

Austen-Leigh concludes his chapter on his aunt by saying, "She was, in fact, as ready to comfort the unhappy, or to nurse the sick, as she was to laugh and jest with the lighthearted."

Meanwhile, scholars have pointed to situations and lines in Austen's novels and comments in her letters to Cassandra that, they say, make it hard to believe that Jane was always sweet, charming, and good natured. In *Pride and Prejudice*, Elizabeth says to her sister, "There are few people whom I really love, and still fewer of whom I think well. The more I see of the world, the more am I dissatisfied with it." In one of her letters to Cassandra, she writes: "Mrs. Hall, of Sherborne, was brought to bed yesterday of a dead child, some weeks before she expected, owing to a fright. I suppose she happened unawares to look at her husband." From another letter: "Mrs. Portman is not much admired in Dorchester; the good-natured world, as usual, extolled her beauty so highly, that all the neighbourhood have had the pleasure of being disappointed." Another letter says, of a maid apprenticed to a dressmaker, "we may hope to see her able to spoil gowns in a few years." She tells her sister that a neighbor's wife is "discovered to be everything that the Neighbourhood could wish her, silly & cross as well as extravagant." She writes that an upcoming ball will probably be "very stupid, there will be nobody worth dancing with, and nobody worth talking to."

Examples like these appear throughout Austen's writing, even in the Juvenalia, and their frequency raises questions about the extent to which sarcastic and cynical comments reveal Austen's personality. Critic Marvin Mudrick says of Jane's youthful writing that she has "close observation without sympathy, common sense without tenderness, densely imagined representation without passion." British novelist Virginia Woolf thinks that Jane Austen "had few illusions about other people and none about herself." Of *Sense and Sensibility*, Halperin comments, "The world of this tale is a dark, dark place, populated by the most astonishing cast of villainous characters assembled by the novelist in any of her books." Of the same book, Virginia Woolf remarks, "it seems as if her creatures were born merely to give Jane Austen the supreme delight of slicing their heads off."

Explanations for the sarcasm and cynicism vary widely. Perhaps Austen used sarcasm as a defense and poked fun so that she did not despair over the evil and foolishness she saw in society. Perhaps Austen, like other satirists, found laughter a better technique for reform than complaint. If her style does indeed reflect real anger and bitterness, Austen's situation perhaps explains it. She was a bright, educated woman with ambition to become a serious novelist, but she lived in a society that imposed strict expectations and limitations on women. Knowing that she had no income and would have no inheritance, she was faced with finding a husband or having to depend on others for her keep. In Austen's time, the oldest child inherited the estate of the parents.

David Cecil takes all of the speculation about meaning less seriously. He comments:

> Jane Austen was always to delight in her fools: without compunction she mocks their follies so as to get all the amusement out of them she can. But, just because she enjoyed them so much, they do not put her out of temper; rather she recognizes them as an addition to the pleasures of life. This was true of her at seventeen as at thirty. . . . The outstanding characteristic of these early works is their rollicking high spirits. From these alone we could deduce that the young Jane Austen enjoyed her existence.

Nevertheless, her enjoyable existence in Steventon came to an abrupt end in 1801 when George Austen retired and moved his wife and daughters to Bath. In November 1800, Jane returned home with her friend Martha Lloyd to find Mrs. Austen at the door announcing, "Well, girls! it is all settled. We have decided to leave Steventon and go to Bath." Though Jane was not ordinarily overwhelmed, at this news she fainted in the doorway. She was deeply attached to Steventon. Austen-Leigh points out that

> this was the residence of Jane Austen for twenty-five years. This was the cradle of her genius. These were the first objects which inspired her young heart with a sense of the beauties of nature. In strolls along those wood-walks, thick-coming fancies rose in her mind, and gradually assumed the forms in which they came forth to the world. In that simple church she brought them all into subjection to the piety which ruled her in life.

Jane had never liked Bath, but by the time of the move in 1801, she was resigned and at least outwardly cheerful. She was unhappy, however, when the family sold five hundred books and Jane's pianoforte because their new quarters were smaller. The heroine in *Persuasion*, a novel Jane wrote in 1816, has a similar experience in which she is forced to leave a home she loves and move to Bath.

Before settling in their new home in the city, George Austen took his wife and daughters on a six-week vacation by the sea, visiting several resorts along the coast. At one of them, Jane had a brief romance. After years of waiting, she found a man she could love and respect, and her family approved of the match. It appears the man had to leave the party for a while but planned to rejoin them later in the vacation. Then Jane received news from his brother that her suitor had died suddenly. Nothing is known about the man besides family gossip, not even his name. As is the case during other periods of troubled emotions, no letters remain, this time for a period of three years.

ROOTLESS YEARS IN BATH AND SOUTHAMPTON

The Austens returned to Bath in the fall, and Jane spent five troubled years in the city. In 1802, while Jane and Cassandra were visiting the Bigg-Withers at their home, Manydown, near Steventon, Harris, the youngest son and heir to the estate, proposed marriage to Jane and she accepted. He was twenty-one and she twenty-six, considered at that time the beginning of middle age. During the night, she realized she could not marry a man she did not love just to have a suitable husband, and in the morning, she broke the engagement. Distressed and embarrassed, she and Cassandra went to her brother at Steventon and insisted on his taking them to Bath immediately. A second disappointment came in 1803, when she sold *Susan* to the publisher who advertised but never published the book. And in 1804, Jane suffered the loss of her good friend and adviser, Mrs. Anne Lefroy, who was killed in a fall from a horse.

The most serious loss was her father's death. In January 1805, after a two-day illness, George Austen died and was buried in a crypt in Walcot, the Bath church where he was married. His death was particularly upsetting to Jane, who loved her father and got on well with him; in contrast, her relationship with her mother was uneasy and often filled with stress. Now the three women were alone and without money. Each of the Austen brothers responded with a £50 annual stipend, and Cassandra could count on interest income from the money her fiance had left her, but Jane had nothing. In the summer of 1805, Jane's unmarried friend, Martha Lloyd, left homeless at the death of her mother, came to live with them. These four women lived together for the rest of Jane's life.

In 1804 and 1805 while living in Bath, Jane tried to write but with little success. She recast *Lady Susan*, a very early epistolary novel written in 1793 or 1794, into story form. The book is a dark tale of the proud, greedy, dishonest Lady Susan, who hates her own daughter. Austen's characters were modeled on people she had only heard about, in a social setting she was acquainted with but had not inhabited. She never tried to publish this novel and never again tried to write about what she did not know firsthand. Then she began *The Watsons*, a realistic and ironic study of women's place in society, a novel that discusses four sisters in search of husbands. The story has a dark tone and portrays women's lives as unfulfilling, devoid of security or happiness; she portrays men as inconstant, vain, and materialistic. After sixty thousand words, she abandoned the novel. Both of these unfinished pieces were published posthumously in 1870 with Austen-Leigh's *Memoir.*

Early in 1806 the decision was made that the women would leave Bath—a decision that particularly pleased Jane—and accept Frank Austen's invitation to live with him and his new wife, Mary, in Southampton. Late in the summer, the newlyweds and the four women moved into a large house at 2 Castle Square in Southampton where they lived until 1809. Little of significance happened in Jane's life during these years in Southampton. She received invitations for morning visits, dinners, card playing, and even an occasional ball, but her letters describe day-to-day events with little enthusiasm and only a sprinkling of the wit found in her earlier letters. In one letter to Cassandra, she said, "I see nothing to be glad of." Martha Lloyd's presence in the household provided another person to care for Mrs. Austen in her declining health and give Jane and Cassandra more opportunity to travel.

On a trip in the summer of 1808 to visit her brother Edward at Godmersham Park in Kent, Austen twice stopped in London to see plays and visit art galleries, both favorite activities. While in Kent, she received another proposal, this one from Edward's brother-in-law, Edward Bridges, a clergyman four years younger than Jane, who was thirty-two. Again she turned down the opportunity for marriage because she did not love the man, but apparently she handled this refusal more gracefully than that to Harris Bigg-Withers. Later that same summer, Cassandra went to Godmersham Park for several weeks to help Edward's wife, Elizabeth, before the birth of her eleventh child. Tragically, ten days after the child's birth, Elizabeth died. (All of Jane's brothers lost their first wives, and only Edward never remarried.) Though Cassandra stayed on to help with the children after Elizabeth's death, Jane, reputed to be concerned, caring, and helpful, volunteered only to care for two of the boys during their brief visit to Southampton.

A HOME IN CHAWTON

By 1809, Edward had inherited the Knight estate: Godmersham Park and the Knight Hampshire houses that George Austen had overseen in Chawton. Edward offered the cottage to his mother, sisters, and Martha Lloyd and kept the great house for himself and his children for their visits there. Chawton is a small village, a mile from the larger village of

Alton, and fifteen miles from Winchester and from Jane's former home in Steventon. The four woman moved into the Chawton cottage on July 7, 1809. Within three weeks, Jane sent a light-hearted poem to her brother Frank about the "many comforts" of their Chawton home, rejoicing that with the completion of the remodeling "It will all other Houses beat." Clearly, Jane was happy to have a secure home and to return to a small village.

The cottage, a two-story brick house with a tiled roof, is hardly spectacular; now, restored, it serves as a museum for manuscripts, documents, and objects from the lives of Jane and her relatives. Perhaps formerly an inn, it stands adjacent to the road between London and Winchester. The sitting rooms, kitchen, and offices are on the first floor of the L-shaped house, and the second floor comprises six bedrooms, enough for the Austen women, Martha Lloyd, servants, and visitors (Jane and Cassandra shared one of the bedrooms). A bake house and a shed for their donkey and cart stand out back, and flower and vegetable gardens, orchards, and hedged walks surround the buildings.

Most of the housekeeping at Chawton fell to Jane and Cassandra since Mrs. Austen, now seventy, devoted her time to gardening and embroidery. Jane was responsible for the winemaking and helped with the gardening and cooking. The women often spent evenings making quilts together. On a typical day, Jane arose early and practiced on her new pianoforte before she made breakfast. Afternoons she spent walking in the gardens or along the hedges, doing errands in Alton, or visiting neighbors. For her private amusement, she made music books of pieces to practice; she wrote them out by drawing the lines by hand and neatly making every note with pen and ink. And secretly she wrote, at a small table with a piece of blotting paper in front of her; if someone came, she quickly hid the manuscript under it. Likewise, she refused to oil a squeaky door, which served as a warning of someone's approach, giving her time to hide her work. Her brother James likened her to some little bird who "builds of the materials nearest at hand, of the twigs and mosses supplied by the tree in which it is placed: curiously constructed out of the simplest matters." She was now seen always wearing her white muslin cap, the sign of a woman in middle age. David Cecil explains : "Indeed her establishment at Chawton marks the turning point in her story. Nothing more was to happen to Jane Austen the woman; from now on her history is that of Jane Austen the artist."

PUBLICATION OF AUSTEN'S EARLY NOVELS

Beginning in 1810, Jane stayed home and secretly worked on her writing. She revised *Sense and Sensibility* and *Pride and Prejudice*, but she could do nothing with *Susan* while the publisher Crosby held the manuscript. Fearing another rejection of *Pride and Prejudice*, she chose to submit the manuscript for *Sense and Sensibility* to a publisher first. Her brother Henry, the banker who lived in London, served as her literary agent, and Thomas Egerton of the Military Library, Whitehall, agreed to publish *Sense and Sensibility* at the author's risk; that is, Jane had to sign an agreement to reimburse the publisher for all losses. While waiting between acceptance and publication, she wrote, "I am never too busy to think of *S&S*. I can no more forget it, than a mother can forget her sucking child." She started immediately to save money, but the thousand copies of the first edition, which came out in November 1811, sold out in twenty months. The book's sale not only covered the costs of publication, but also earned £140 for Jane, considerably increased by the sales of the second edition.

Only the most intimate family members knew that Jane was a published author; the title page of *Sense and Sensibility* said "By a Lady." One day when Jane was in the Alton library with her niece Anna, Jane casually pointed out *Sense and Sensibility* as one of the books newly arrived from London. Anna picked it up, looked at the cover, and said, "With a title like that it must be rubbish," and put it down. Encouraged by the success of her first publication, Jane risked submitting *Pride and Prejudice* again. She wanted £150, but Egerton offered to pay £110, and she took his offer. *Pride and Prejudice* appeared in January 1813 "By the Author of *Sense and Sensibility*." When the newly published copies arrived, Jane wrote, "I have got my own darling child from London. . . . I must confess that I think her [Elizabeth] as delightful a creature as ever appeared in print, and how I shall be able to tolerate those who do not like *her* . . . I do not know." *Pride and Prejudice* was an immediately success, soon a popular topic of dinner-table conversation and the object of critics' praise. Jane's nephew James-Edward read and enjoyed both of the published novels without knowing that his aunt was the author.

THREE NEW NOVELS

Jane began to write *Mansfield Park* in 1812 and completed the rough draft by July 1813, revising until late into December. A mature woman now, Austen addresses the deeper subjects of social changes emerging in England and the moral and immoral perceptions about events and behavior. Its main character is the unassuming but courageous Fanny Price, many readers' favorite Austen heroine. Egerton published the book in May 1814, "By the Author of *Sense and Sensibility* and *Pride and Prejudice*," and the initial fifteen hundred copies sold within six months. For financial advantages, Henry arranged for a second publisher to issue the second edition of the *Mansfield Park*, but the book did not continue to sell well. About this time, her brother leaked the secret of her identity. Though sworn not to divulge any information about his sister's authorship, he could not resist dropping hints when London readers speculated about who the author might be. When, finally, the news was out, Jane said of her new-found fame, "What a trifle it all is to the really important points of one's existence."

Jane's next novel, *Emma*, took her fourteen months to write, from the beginning of January 1814 to the end of March 1815; it was published on her fortieth birthday, December 16, 1815. After a series of coincidences, Jane dedicated this novel to England's prince regent, the future George IV. Jane was in London nursing her brother Henry through a serious illness, about which his physician, Charles Thomas Haden, consulted a colleague who happened to be one of the prince's personal physicians. By this time Jane was well known, and the physician mentioned that the prince liked Jane's books and kept a set in each of his residences. Through the grapevine, the prince learned that his physician saw Jane Austen regularly at her brother's bedside. The prince directed his librarian and chaplain, James Stanier Clarke, to call on her and invite her to tour Carlton House, one of the prince's residences. During her visit on November 13, 1815, Clarke informed her that she was free to dedicate her next book to the prince. Jane, however, strongly disapproved of the future king and planned to ignore the invitation. Through correspondence, Jane learned, however, that being "free to" really meant that she was "expected to." So she dedicated *Emma* to the future George IV "By His Royal Highness's Permission, Most Respectfully," by "His Royal Highness's Dutiful and Obedient Humble Servant, the Author." Austen and the publisher honored the prince with special copies bound in red.

Three months after she had completed *Emma*, Jane began writing *Persuasion*, which she worked on through the winter months. The financial success of *Emma* allowed her to buy back the manuscript of *Susan* from Crosby, but she had to be discreet to keep him from finding out that he owned a manuscript by the author of four successful novels. Jane enlisted

Henry as her agent, and he secured the manuscript before he told the astonished publisher that Jane Austen was the author. In the spring of 1816, Jane was occupied with three projects: finishing *Persuasion*, revising *Susan*, and writing "Plan of a Novel," a burlesque on romantic fiction. She completed the burlesque in the spring, finished the final revisions of *Persuasion* on August 6, changed the title of *Susan* to *Northanger Abbey* and the name of the heroine to Catherine and then put it on the shelf. *Persuasion* and *Northanger Abbey* were published together the year after Jane's death.

FAILING HEALTH

By the time she finished *Persuasion*, Jane was desperately ill. She had a form of tuberculosis that attacked the adrenal glands. At that time, the disease had no name; it was named Addison's Disease in 1849, and today it is treated with cortisone. Its symptoms are blotchy skin, erratic body temperature, low blood pressure, nausea, and vomiting. Jane became weaker by stages: When she could no longer walk to Alton, she rode the donkey; when riding the donkey was too taxing, she rode in the cart. Finally, she spent most of her days lying on a couch made by arranging two or three chairs. Yet she kept writing, and her letters to relatives repeatedly note that she thought she was getting better. On January 29, 1817, she began another book entitled *Sandition*. It is an attack on improvers and developers who flaunt tradition and destroy the countryside. By March 18, she had written twenty-five thousand words, but could write no more. Except for a half-dozen letters, her work on *Sandition*, not published until 1925, was her last writing.

On April 27, 1817, Austen made a will, leaving all of her money to Cassandra, except for £50 bequeathed to Henry's housekeeper, who had lost money when Henry's bank failed. She left a necklace to Louisa Knight and a lock of her hair to her favorite niece, Fanny. Because her doctor lived in Winchester, the family moved her there to be closer to his care. On May 24, the carriage came from Steventon and, in a downpour, took Jane and Cassandra to lodgings in Winchester. Her brother Henry and Edward Knight's nineteen-year-old son, William, rode on horseback, one on each side. Cassandra nursed Jane as her health deteriorated rapidly. Early in the morning of Friday, July 18, the end near, Cassandra asked Jane if she wanted anything, and Jane replied: "Nothing but death, God grant me patience, Pray for me oh pray for me." Medicated, she was soon unconscious. She lay with her head on a pillow in Cassandra's lap and died at 4:30 in the morning.

Early in the morning on July 24, Austen was buried in Winchester Cathedral, attended only by three brothers and a nephew. Cassandra watched from the lodging window as bearers carried her body to the church. The family arranged to have her grave marked with a black marble slab and wrote the following inscription for it. It is noteworthy that the inscription makes no mention of her as a novelist.

In Memory of
JANE AUSTEN
youngest daughter of the late
Rev GEORGE AUSTEN
formerly Rector of Steventon in this county
she departed this life on the 18th of July, 1817,
aged 4l, after a long illness supported with
the patience and the hopes of a Christian.

The benevolence of her heart,
the sweetness of her temper, and
the extraordinary endowments of her mind
obtained the regard of all who knew her, and
the warmest love of her intimate connections.

Their grief is in proportion to their affection
They know their loss to be irreparable
but in their deepest affliction they are consoled
by a firm though humble hope that her charity,
devotion, faith and purity have rendered
her soul acceptable in the sight of her
REDEEMER

In the middle of the nineteenth century, one of the vergers in Winchester Cathedral wondered why so many people asked for directions to Jane Austen's grave. "Was there," he asked, "anything particular about that lady?" In 1872 a brass tablet was added on the north wall of the Cathedral near her grave. It says

JANE AUSTEN

known to many by her writings,
endeared to her family
by the varied charms of her Character
and ennobled by Christian faith and piety,
was born at Steventon in the County of Hants.
Dec. xvi mdcclxxv,
and buried in this Cathedral
July xxiv mdcccxvii

"She opened her mouth with wisdom
and in her tongue is the law of
kindness."

Prov. xxxi. v. xxvi

CHAPTER 1

Major Themes

READINGS ON
PRIDE AND PREJUDICE

Marriage and Manners in a Civilized Society

Bernard J. Paris

Bernard J. Paris's analysis of marriage and manners in *Pride and Prejudice* sheds light on their meaning for the individual in a highly formal society. Paris identifies characters whose attitudes are either too focused on the self or too artificially proper. He argues that Austen, while advocating the proper blend between extremes that Elizabeth and Darcy achieve, also shows the pitfalls in communicating strictly through the practice of proper manners. While teaching English at Michigan State University at East Lansing, Bernard J. Paris was granted a Guggenheim fellowship to study Jane Austen; he has also taught at the University of Florida at Gainesville. He is the author of *Experiments in Life: George Eliot's Quest for Values* and *A Psychological Approach to Fiction: Studies in Stendhal, George Eliot, Dostoevsky, and Conrad.*

Pride and Prejudice is Jane Austen's most sophisticated exploration of the relationship between the individual and society. In her treatment of marriage, of manners, and of various other aspects of our personal and communal lives, she attempts to strike a delicate balance between the necessity of prudence, decorum, and social responsibility on the one hand, and the desirability of self-expression, spontaneity, and personal fulfillment on the other. She gives the institutions, values, and conventions of the established order all due respect; but she shows at the same time that they are subject to distortion and can stand in the way of happiness, sincerity, and truth. Individualism, too, has its dangers, as she is always careful to show. Her satire is directed against an excessive emphasis upon either set of considerations. Her object in this novel is to explore the possibilities of combining the

Reprinted from Bernard J. Paris, *Character and Conflict in Jane Austen's Novels: A Psychological Approach* (Detroit: Wayne State University Press, 1978), by permission of the author.

requirements of social life with legitimate aspirations for personal integrity and satisfaction.

MARRIAGE AS A PERSONAL RELATIONSHIP AND A SOCIAL INSTITUTION

Marriage is an ideal vehicle for Jane Austen's thematic concerns. It is at once a personal relationship and a social institution, and both of its aspects are important. Austen feels that one should marry for love, for personal satisfaction, and out of a regard for the human qualities of one's partner. At the same time, one cannot ignore the socioeconomic position of the other person. Mrs. Gardiner warns Elizabeth against becoming involved with Wickham, and Elizabeth accepts her advice. Attractive as Wickham seems to be at this time, he is not an eligible mate for a woman like Elizabeth, who has almost no personal fortune and whose family lives under the threat of an entail.[1] In a similar way, Colonel Fitzwilliam finds Elizabeth attractive; but he lets her know that he must marry a woman with money. Neither Elizabeth nor Colonel Fitzwilliam would marry *for* money, but they must hope to fall in love with someone who *has* money. They are wise to avoid emotional involvement with people who are unsuitable from a prudential point of view, however attractive they may be personally.

People cannot always fall in love where they choose, but their choice of a marriage partner should not be governed primarily by concerns for money or status. There are many examples of possible or endangered connections which illustrate the potential evil of sacrificing personal preference to social or economic considerations. Elizabeth cannot forget about the entail, but she should not marry Collins because of it. She is tolerant of Wickham's attentions to Miss King only as long as she thinks that he might care for her. Other possible marriages which illustrate this point are those of Darcy and Lady Anne, Darcy and Miss Bingley, and Bingley and Georgiana. There is no personal attraction in any of these relationships, but the marriages are desired out of personal ambition or to enhance the wealth and status of the families. The endangered connections are those of Elizabeth with Darcy and Jane with Bingley.

It is true, as many critics have observed, that *Pride and*

---

1. a predetermined order of succession, as to an estate

Prejudice evokes a vision of society as governed by the values of the marketplace. Human relations, and especially the marriage relation, are threatened by an excessive emphasis upon money and status. It should be noted, however, that this debasement of social institutions and interpersonal relationships is more of a threat and an object of satire than a triumphant reality in the world of the novel. It is exemplified more by possible and endangered connections than by actual ones, and the characters whose values are faulty either turn out to have little power or are reformed.

There is one actual marriage which is motivated solely by socioeconomic considerations—that of Charlotte and Mr. Collins. When Charlotte accepts Collins, Elizabeth feels that she has "sacrificed every better feeling to worldly advantage." We are eventually made to feel, however, not that Charlotte's attitude toward marriage is correct or that she has made a happy choice, but that she has been realistic for herself and has chosen the lesser evil. Jane Austen does not blame her, and even Elizabeth becomes somewhat reconciled to her choice. Charlotte's marriage remains, nonetheless, the darkest note in the novel. This sensitive and intelligent woman has been forced by the accidents of her lot to be cynical about marriage and to prostitute herself for status and security.

ELIZABETH'S AND DARCY'S ATTITUDES TOWARD MARRIAGE

Elizabeth and Darcy tend to crisscross in their attitudes toward marriage in the course of the novel. Neither begins with an extreme position: Elizabeth is somewhat to the left and Darcy somewhat to the right of center. Darcy is attracted to Elizabeth quite early, but he sees the connection as unsuitable to the dignity of his family, and he tries to regulate his feelings accordingly. He is so much in love, however, that he decides to make a social sacrifice for the sake of personal satisfaction. The problem from Elizabeth's point of view is the reverse. However magnificent her prospects as Darcy's wife, she cannot think of marrying him until she comes to care for him personally.

After being at first the chief obstacle to love, Darcy becomes the most romantic figure in the book; and he does this without losing his character as the defender of traditional values. He uses his great power in the service of both order and desire. He combats the anarchistic tendencies of Lydia and Wickham on the one hand and the tyranny of

Lady Catherine on the other. He saves the Bennet family and rescues the heroine from all the sources of her distress. He marries her for love and transports her to the comfort and elegance of Pemberley.

Elizabeth has a regard for the social aspects of marriage, but she seems to represent at the outset a predominantly individualistic point of view. Her change of heart toward Darcy is profoundly influenced, however, by social considerations. She is impressed at Pemberley not only by the grandeur of the estate, but also by the importance of such a man as Darcy, who has so many dependents, and by his obligation to choose wisely in the matter of a wife. Mrs. Reynolds' description of his exemplary behavior in his many social roles impresses Elizabeth quite as much as the information that he has a good temper. Elizabeth's experiences with her father have prepared her to appreciate such evidence of responsibility. When we consider that she finds herself drawn to the idea of being Darcy's wife before her renewed contact with the man himself, we must conclude that Darcy's social attractiveness plays a large part in the awakening of her desire.

There is little doubt that Jane Austen sees the marriage of Darcy and Elizabeth as a union which will "teach the admiring multitude what connubial felicity really" is. The novel aims, through this marriage, at a resolution of the dialectic I have been examining between the social and the personal aspects of marriage. By having each of the protagonists come to appreciate and to be motivated by the other's point of view, while maintaining a concern for his own, Austen seeks to do fullest justice to both sets of values.

PROPER MANNERS REFLECT GENUINE FEELINGS

Pride and Prejudice is as much about manners as it is about marriage. The word "civility" occurs, in one form or another, over seventy times in the novel. It is part of a cluster of frequently recurring terms which includes "manners," "decorum," "propriety," and "politeness." Civilization is based, in part, upon the observance of proper forms of behavior. In a society of highly formal manners, such as that depicted in this novel, there is a prescribed way for each individual to behave in almost every situation of life. Socialization is the process by which the individual learns his place in the world and acquires the manners appropriate to it. Ideally, he learns not only to behave, but also to feel as he ought, so that his manners communicate his true sentiments and reflect his character. In *Pride and Prejudice*, as in all of Austen's novels, individuals tend to be judged in terms of their breeding. Those who are either under- or oversocialized are objects of satire, as are those whose manners are

LYDIA'S INSENSITIVITY AND BAD MANNERS

After eloping with Wickham, Lydia returns to the Bennets with her new husband. As the family gathers for their reception, Lydia chatters inappropriately, confirming Austen's intent to portray her as simple and reckless.

Lydia was Lydia still; untamed, unabashed, wild, noisy, and fearless. She turned from sister to sister, demanding their congratulations, and when at length they all sat down, looked eagerly round the room, took notice of some little alteration in it, and observed, with a laugh, that it was a great while since she had been there. . . .

There was no want of discourse. The bride and her mother could neither of them talk fast enough; and Wickham, who happened to sit near Elizabeth, began enquiring after his acquaintance in that neighbourhood, with a good humoured ease, which she felt very unable to equal in her replies. They seemed each of them to have the happiest memories in the world. Nothing of the past was recollected with pain; and Lydia led voluntarily to subjects, which her sisters would not have alluded to for the world.

"Only think of its being three months," she cried, "since I went away; it seems but a fortnight I declare; and yet there have been things enough happened in the time. Good gracious! when I went away, I am sure I had no more idea of being married till I came back again! though I thought it would be very good fun if I was."

Her father lifted up his eyes. Jane was distressed. Elizabeth looked expressively at Lydia; but she, who never heard nor saw any thing of which she chose to be insensible, gaily continued, "Oh! mamma, do the people here abouts know I am married today? I was afraid they might not; and we overtook William Goulding in his curricle, so I was determined he should know it, and so I let down the side glass next to him, and took off my glove, and let my hand just rest upon the window frame, so that he might see the ring, and then I bowed and smiled like any thing."

Elizabeth could bear it no longer. She got up, and ran out of the room.

Jane Austen, *Pride and Prejudice.*

only a facade which hides their unscrupulous natures. In manners, as in marriage, it is necessary to strike a balance between self-expression and respect for propriety.

Lydia and Collins represent the extremes of lopsided development. Lydia is uncivilized. She is guided by her impulses, which are primitive, and her manners are atrocious. She feels and behaves improperly in every situation and continually gives pain to those around her. The characters who most closely resemble her are her mother and her aunt Philips, both of whom encourage her wildness. Darcy, Lady Catherine, and Mr. Bennet also display self-indulgence in their social behavior. Collins represents the opposite evil. He seems to be nothing but his social mask or persona. His civilities are excessive partly because they have no feeling, no personal sensitivity, behind them. He overdoes what is proper in every situation and is successful only with people who are themselves preoccupied with rituals. His closest counterpart is Sir William Lucas, whose civilities are less excessive but not much more meaningful than his. Bingley, Jane, Elizabeth, and the Gardiners represent a happy combination of feeling and form: they are at once well-bred and genuinely concerned for others. Manners such as theirs, however, can be deceptive. Wickham only appears to be what they are.

Darcy's manners are in need of adjustment. They are at once too formal and too self-indulgent. Darcy's sense of dignity is so great that he has difficulty relating to people, even his intimates, with feeling and spontaneity. Darcy's self-indulgence lies in his indifference to the feelings of those who are not his equals or intimates. His "manners . . . [are] well-bred," but he will not trouble himself to be friendly, and he continually gives offence. His faulty manners result from a flaw in his character. He changes for the better in both feeling and behavior as a consequence of Elizabeth's refusal, which forces him into self-examination: "'I was spoiled by my parents, who . . . allowed, encouraged, almost taught me to be selfish and overbearing, to care for none beyond my own family circle, to think meanly of all the rest of the world.'"

It is Elizabeth who achieves the most delicate balance between the requirements of self and of society. Her manners are easy and playful, but she takes serious things seriously and is careful of the feelings of others. She does not always say what she thinks, but she knows her own mind, and she tries not to mislead or to be forced into a false position by the demands of the occasion. Upon her departure from Hunsford, while Collins engages in a ceremonious leave-taking, Elizabeth tries "to unite civility and truth in a few short sentences." A certain amount of hypocrisy is built into the system, of course. The well-bred person cannot be expected to like or to respect everyone he meets, but he is expected to behave in a gracious way. Elizabeth plays a role, as does everyone else; but she can be extremely direct when others trespass upon her dignity, as Lady Catherine and Darcy learn to their pain. She can also be guided by a benevolent impulse, whatever others may think, as when she walks three miles through mud to visit Jane. Elizabeth is at once a highly individual and a deeply social being, and her manners reflect this synthesis.

CIVIL BEHAVIOR MAY LEAD TO FAULTY COMMUNICATION

Jane Austen clearly appreciates the values of civilization; but she is aware, too, of the pitfalls and limitations of the established order. The code of civility regulates our impulses, provides patterns of interaction, and permits us to come together without continually hurting each other's feelings. At the same time, however, it inhibits self-expression, isolates us from each other, and makes knowledge and communication difficult. It is one of the major blocking forces in the comic action of the novel. Elizabeth and Darcy come together only after there have been major breakdowns of civility.

Skilled as they are in communicating their own feelings and interpreting those of others, the members of this society still make numerous mistakes. The masking effect of social forms combines with personal factors in both the actor and the observer to produce a wide range of misunderstandings. At the time of his first proposal, Darcy believes Elizabeth "'to be wishing, expecting [his] addresses.'" Darcy's arrogance is partly responsible for this gross error, but he has also been misled by Elizabeth, who expresses her dislike under the guise of raillery. "'My manners,'" says Elizabeth, "'must have been at fault, but not intentionally I assure you.'" The reader, who is much better informed than he could be in real life, enjoys the irony not only of Darcy's, but also of Elizabeth's mistakes. In almost every exchange between them in the first half of the novel Darcy and Elizabeth misinterpret each other. He fails to understand her hostile and she his attentive behavior. An equally important failure of communication occurs, of course, between Jane and Bingley. Her manners are so generally agreeable and he is so diffident that Bingley fails to perceive how much he is loved. Their difficulties illustrate a recurring problem in Jane Austen: given the restrictive patterns of courtship and the modest behavior prescribed for women, how are young people to come to an understanding?

Since so much social behavior is a form of acting, it is difficult not only to express and interpret feelings, but also to read character. Miss Bingley is well understood by an astute observer like Elizabeth, but for a long time she deceives Jane. Even Elizabeth, however, is seriously mistaken about Wickham and Darcy. Wickham is a marvelous actor who charms everyone on first acquaintance. Darcy refuses to pretend ("'disguise of every sort is my abhorrence'"); and, as a result, he is highly unpopular. Wickham's "countenance, voice, and manner [establish] him at once in the possession of every virtue"; there is "truth in his looks." Darcy's manner disposes Elizabeth not only to dislike him, but to believe him capable of gross misconduct.

Elizabeth's mistakes are cleared up and communication with Darcy is established by the breakdown of civility which occurs when Darcy proposes. By dwelling upon his sense of Elizabeth's "inferiority—of its being a degradation," Darcy provokes her into a direct revelation of her feelings. Her charges concerning his mistreatment of Wickham and his interference with Jane and Bingley set in motion the chain of events, beginning with Darcy's letter, which eventually removes most of the obstacles to the happy ending. The most serious charge which Elizabeth makes, from Darcy's point of view, is that he behaves in an ungentleman-like manner. This criticism stings him to the core; he has always prided himself on being well-bred.

By the time of Darcy's second proposal, both parties are ashamed of their past conduct. Elizabeth accuses herself of having "'abused [him] so abominably to [his] face.'"

> "What did you say to me [replied Darcy], that I did not deserve. . . . my behavior to you at the time, had merited the severest reproof. It was unpardonable. I cannot think of it without abhorrence."
>
> "We will not quarrel for the greater share of blame annexed to that evening," said Elizabeth. "The conduct of neither, if strictly examined, will be irreproachable; but since then, we have both, I hope, improved in civility."

What Elizabeth says is true; both were indecorous that evening, though her conduct was provoked by his, and she is now being gracious in accepting an equal share of the blame. The irony is that if they had both remained civil, they would never have come to know each other or themselves; and neither their marriage nor that of Jane and Bingley would have taken place.

The final resolution is facilitated by two further violations of decorum. When they meet at Pemberley, Darcy tries to show through his manners that he has changed and that he is still interested in Elizabeth; and Elizabeth tries to be responsive without seeming forward. They separate, however, under adverse conditions (Lydia has run off with Wickham); and each is in doubt about the feelings of the other. The first breakthrough in communication occurs when Lydia reveals, in her characteristically reckless way, the secret of Darcy's presence at her marriage. Since the confidence has already been broken, Mrs. Gardiner can now disclose the full extent of Darcy's assistance to the family; and this encourages Elizabeth to believe that he may still love her. The second violation of decorum is Lady Catherine's attempt to coerce Elizabeth into promising that she will never marry her nephew. Here, as in the first proposal scene, Elizabeth is extremely outspoken. Lady Catherine's report of this conversation, which is intended to discourage Darcy's interest, has the opposite effect and leads to the second proposal: "'It taught me to hope . . . as I had scarcely ever allowed myself to hope before. I knew enough of your disposition to be certain, that, had you been absolutely, irrevocably decided against me, you would have acknowledged it to Lady Catherine, frankly and openly.'" Elizabeth's earlier frankness, which Darcy had felt to be uncivil, now gives him confidence in his interpretation of her behavior.

Social Moderation and the Middle Way

Alistair M. Duckworth

Alistair M. Duckworth argues that in *Pride and Prejudice* Jane Austen advocates middle ground between individualism and traditional social conventions as the best way to bridge separations between individuals and between social classes. Duckworth follows Elizabeth's changing attitudes throughout the book, until she finally reflects on herself and Darcy with thoughtful understanding. When the couple finds middle ground between their original extremes, their marriage symbolizes a synthesis of Austen's fictional world. Alistair Duckworth has taught at the University of Virginia, the State University of New York in Buffalo, and the University of Florida. He is a contributor to *Jane Austen: Bicentenary Essays.*

More successfully than *Sense and Sensibility, Pride and Prejudice* moves from an initial condition of potential social fragmentation to a resolution in which the grounds of society are reconstituted as the principal characters come together in marriage. As in the former novel, there is a recognition of widespread economic motivation in human conduct, but a more important bar, initially, to the continuity of a traditionally grounded society is the existence everywhere of separations—between classes in the context of society as a whole, between minds in the smaller context of the home.

The fragmentary nature of the novel's world is humorously evident from the beginning in the constitution of the Bennet family itself, as any number of scenes could illustrate. . . . The distances of the drawing room, moreover, are the mirror of social distances outside. As a "gulf impassable" seems to loom between Darcy and Elizabeth, so there are seemingly uncrossable distances between the aristocracy

From Alistair M. Duckworth, *The Improvement of the Estate: A Study of Jane Austen's Novels,* pp. 116, 117–26, 132, 142, 143. Copyright © 1971 by The Johns Hopkins University Press. Reprinted by permission of the author and The Johns Hopkins University Press.

(Darcy and Lady Catherine), the gentry (the Bennets), and "trade" (the Phillipses and the Gardiners). Those who were "formerly in trade"—the Lucases and the Bingleys—add mobility, but hardly continuity, to the social moment, as they seek landed security at their different levels.

How in this world of distances are people, and classes, to come together? This, the crucial question underlying *Pride and Prejudice*, is answered primarily through the education of the hero and heroine, whose union is not only to their mutual advantage, but brings together widely separate outlooks and social positions. As many critics have argued, it is in the mutuality of the concessions made by Elizabeth and Darcy that the novel's attraction lies. If Elizabeth's private vision is shown to be insufficient, then so, too, is Darcy's arrogant assumption that status is value-laden. Only when Elizabeth recognizes that individualism must find its social limits, and Darcy concedes that tradition without individual energy is empty form, can the novel reach its eminently satisfactory conclusion.

That Darcy's pride is convincingly humiliated needs little documentation, but it is more important, I think, to consider Elizabeth's education in the novel. Hers is the only mind to which we are granted continual access, and through her internal development from a private to a social outlook we discover again that for Jane Austen an individual's moral duty is necessarily to society, properly understood, and that any retreat into a subjective morality is misguided. While *Pride and Prejudice* quite clearly looks with a critical eye upon automatic social responses, it also validates inherited social principles as they are made relevant to the conditions of the moment and properly informed by individual commitment. To support this argument, it will be necessary, first, to demonstrate how carefully Jane Austen has qualified Elizabeth's largely admirable individualism.

ELIZABETH'S STRONG INDIVIDUALISM

For a long time the inadequacy of the heroine's outlook is concealed, as the narrative strategy emphasizes its undoubted virtues. Elizabeth's morality, when seen in action, is praiseworthy. On learning that her sister is ill at Netherfield, and discovering that the carriage is not to be had, she walks the three miles to Bingley's house, "jumping over stiles and springing over puddles with impatient activity, and finding herself at last within view of the house, with weary ancles, dirty stockings, and a face glowing with the warmth of exercise." Clearly, the context of Elizabeth's morality is personal. What is important to her are friendship and love, the mutual reciprocation of kindness and concern by two people— sisters, lovers, or friends. This present, all is excusable; this absent, nothing is. But the very reduction of the area of her moral concern renders her outlook susceptible, for, if the other in a close relationship fails to reciprocate affection or trust, disappointment must ensue. A common theme in the eighteenth century novel treats the withdrawal of the idealist, disappointed in friendship or love, into misanthropy. . . . And at one point in the novel Elizabeth seems about to follow in this tradition: "The more I see of the world, the more am I dissatisfied with it; and every day confirms my belief of the inconsistency of all human characters, and of the little dependence that can be placed on the appearance of either merit or sense." Like many eighteenth century figures, Elizabeth has been misled by "appearance": Bingley, who seemed about to propose to Jane, has left Netherfield for London without declaring himself; and Charlotte Lucas, who ought to have had more "sense," has accepted Collins's proposal of marriage. Justified as Elizabeth seems to be in her censure of "inconsistency" in these two cases, her outlook has nevertheless been shown incapable of distinguishing appearance from reality—and in a heroine whose most laudable characteristic has been considered her "discrimination," this is surely matter for comment.

THE DIFFICULTY OF PERCEIVING BEYOND APPEARANCES

Elizabeth's experience with Wickham, of course, reveals this inadequacy even more clearly. Like Willoughby, Wickham is at first view "most gentlemanlike"; "he had all the best part of beauty, a fine countenance, a good figure, and very pleasing address." But these are external qualities only, and it is significant that we hear nothing of his "character," "understanding," "mind"—the inner qualities which Jane Austen invariably requires to inform the outward show. As Elizabeth herself will later realize, the "impropriety" of Wickham's communications at a first meeting is blatant; but, already prejudiced against Darcy, she accepts Wickham's slanderous perspective, and in later refusing Darcy's proposal of marriage will adduce as a major reason his treatment of Wickham: "In what imaginary act of *friendship* can you here defend yourself?" (my italics).

Wickham, it seems to Elizabeth initially, like herself and Jane, holds brief for the holiness of the heart's affections. He discovers value, so it appears, in friendship or in the spontaneous action of the self, and not in a conformity to sterile social principles. In this way, he is the opposite of Darcy, who, in Elizabeth's eyes, allows "nothing for the influence of friendship and affection." Thus, when Jane wishes to see both Wickham and Darcy as in some way right—"do but consider in what a disgraceful light it places Mr. Darcy"—Elizabeth refuses to be persuaded that Wickham's view is just another perspective on Darcy's character. "There was truth in his looks," she says of Wickham, "one knows exactly what to think." And at the Netherfield Ball which follows, although it is Wickham and not Darcy who is absent—in spite of the former's assertion that he has "no reason for avoiding" Darcy—it is against Darcy that Elizabeth's "feeling of displeasure" is directed.

In accepting Wickham at face value, Elizabeth repeats the folly of the naive protagonist in the eighteenth century novel. And she has yet to learn the lesson that "as for faces—you may look into them to know whether a man's nose be a long or a short one."[1] But beyond the inherited theme of appearance versus reality, there is in *Pride and Prejudice* an additional awareness of the difficulties involved in reaching a true interpretation of any character. Even without bias, different people will respond to a particular person in different ways—as the Bennet family variously react to Mr Collins's letter. It may also be that no individual is the same from one day to the next. As [critic] Reuben Brower has shown, a sense of the relativity of interpretation and of the variability of character is central to *Pride and Prejudice*. . . . The possibility is presented and then withdrawn, and through Elizabeth's education in this matter we learn how relativity can be excluded from social relations and from a moral outlook.

The relativistic (or better, perspectivistic) aspects involved in knowing another person are touched upon at the Netherfield Ball, where a conversation between Elizabeth and Darcy reveals the extent to which initial interpretations

---

1. The advice given to, but not of course taken by, Harley in Henry Mackenzie's *The Man of Feeling* (1771). Cf. too, Parson Adams's naïve defense of physiognomy in *Joseph Andrews*, refuted by the innkeeper who was formerly a sea captain (in Bk. II, chap. 17).

of character are constructions, or sketches, based on available (and often inadequate) information. When Elizabeth accuses Darcy of "an unsocial, taciturn disposition," he concedes that this may be a "faithful portrait" in her eyes; and when Elizabeth later questions him about his "temper," she admits that her questions are intended to provide an "illustration" of his character. Darcy has earlier been made aware of her meeting with Wickham, a fact that has bearing on the following exchange:

> She shook her head. "I do not get on at all. I hear such different accounts of you as puzzle me exceedingly."
> "I can readily believe," answered he gravely, "that report may vary greatly with respect to me; and I could wish, Miss Bennet, that you were not to sketch my character at the present moment, as there is reason to fear that the performance would reflect no credit on either."
> "But if I do not take your likeness now, I may never have another opportunity."

Darcy is here suggesting that Elizabeth should avoid basing her judgment of him on "report," whether the general report of Meryton or the particular report of Wickham. In either case the sketch she will draw will be partial, for its perspective will be limited. Darcy's true character is not to be immediately derived, as Wickham's character has been by Elizabeth, from external appearances. Unwilling to accede to Darcy's implied request that she postpone her judgment, however, Elizabeth takes his likeness now. Her decision angers Darcy, and they part, not to meet again until they come together at Hunsford.

ELIZABETH'S PERSPECTIVE UNDERGOES CHANGE

There, in his letter to her following her rejection of his proposal, Elizabeth begins to see Darcy's character in a different "light" and to recognize how badly she has misjudged him from a too easy acceptance of Wickham's partial view and a too hasty response to externals—"every charm of air and address." The perspectivist theme is more importantly continued in the second great recognition scene, Elizabeth's visit to Pemberley. At Darcy's estate Elizabeth comes to an awareness of Darcy's intrinsically worthy character and of the deficiencies of her own outlook. Taken with her response to his letter, her visit to Derbyshire marks a crucial change in the direction of her critical views, which now turn inward on herself and her family, at the same time as her ethical outlook broadens to take in other than personal and interpersonal factors. At first, Pemberley seems only to add contradictory perspectives on the man; but on larger view the visit refutes perspectivism as a bar to true moral discrimination, as it recognizes its inevitable existence in human relations.

Mrs. Reynolds, the Pemberley housekeeper, is the source of new views of both Darcy and Wickham. In his housekeeper's eyes, Darcy is nothing less than "the best landlord, and the best master . . . that ever lived." Wickham's previous grudging concessions of Darcy's landed and familial pride take on different import in the "amiable light" of Mrs. Reynolds's representation. But Elizabeth's discovery of a portrait of Darcy in the picture gallery provides the most radical change of perspective. It is fitting that Elizabeth, the "natural" character, who knows "nothing of the art," should come upon this artistic representation of Darcy. Pictured "with such a smile over the face," Darcy appears differently from her own previous "illustration" of him as "unsocial" and "taciturn." Taken with the housekeeper's freely offered information that Darcy had been the "sweetest-tempered, most generous-hearted" of children, this "striking resemblance" can only provide food for "contemplation": "as she stood before the canvas, on which he was represented, and fixed his eyes upon herself, she thought of his regard with a deeper sentiment of gratitude than it had ever raised before; she remembered its warmth, and softened its impropriety of expression." Noticeably, she does not so much look at Darcy in the picture, as have him look at her; she "fixed his eyes upon herself." Now she tries to see herself from Darcy's vantage point, and it is therefore appropriate that, soon after, when Darcy unexpectedly comes upon her in the grounds, she should recognize "in what a disgraceful light" *she* must now appear to him.

At Pemberley, Darcy is "so desirous to please, so free from self-consequence" that had she and the Gardiners "drawn his character from their own feelings, and his servant's report, without any reference to any other account, the circle in Hertfordshire to which he was known, would not have recognised it for Mr. Darcy."[2] In his home Darcy is exemplary, and the description of his estate, though general, is a natural analogue of his social and moral character.

2. Mrs. Reynolds is not, however, without "family prejudice," and Jane Austen is careful to provide more than one view of Darcy even at Pemberley. The Lambton community view has "nothing to accuse him of but pride"; but they also acknowledge his liberality and charity.

Pemberley is a model estate, possessing those indications of value that Jane Austen everywhere provides in her descriptions of properly run estates—beautiful trees, well-disposed landscapes, a handsome house, and finely proportioned rooms. Its grounds, while aesthetically pleasing, are quite without pretension or evidence of extravagance. There is a kind of scenic *mediocritas*[3] about the estate, a mean between the extremes of the improver's art and uncultivated nature:

> It was a large, handsome, stone building, standing well on rising ground, and backed by a ridge of high woody hills;—and in front, a stream of some natural importance was swelled into greater, but without any artificial appearance. Its banks were neither formal, nor falsely adorned. Elizabeth was delighted. She had never seen a place for which nature had done more, or where natural beauty had been so little counteracted by an awkward taste.

ELIZABETH'S NEW PERSPECTIVE

... Thus, when Elizabeth comes to exclaim to herself that "to be mistress of Pemberley might be something," she has, we might conjecture, come to recognize not merely the money and the status of Pemberley, but its value as the setting of a traditional social and ethical orientation, its possibilities—seemingly now only hypothetical—as a context for her responsible social activity.

Following Elizabeth's journey through the park the perspectivist theme is interestingly continued as she accompanies the housekeeper into the dining parlor:

> It was a large, well-proportioned room, handsomely fitted up. Elizabeth, after slightly surveying it, went to a window to enjoy its prospect. The hill, crowned with wood, from which they had descended, receiving increased abruptness from the distance, was a beautiful object. Every disposition of the ground was good; and she looked on the whole scene, the river, the trees scattered on its banks, and the winding of the valley, as far as she could trace it, with delight. As they passed into other rooms, these objects were taking different positions; but from every window there were beauties to be seen.

By looking through the dining parlor window, Elizabeth sees the "whole scene" from one point of view and "as far as she could trace it." She recognizes the harmony of the scene with delight. As she moves from room to room, however, the "objects were taking different positions." "Nevertheless, it is still the

3. moderation

same landscape that she views. Her position, not the disposition of the ground, is what has altered. By traveling first through the park, then by looking back over it, Elizabeth is made aware of the permanence of the estate and yet of the necessarily partial and angled view of the individual. She sees that no overall view is possible to the single vision, but that an approximation to such a view is possible provided the individual is both retrospective and circumspect. More than this, it is not only the angle of the view but the distance from the object which renders the individual sight fallible. An abrupt hill may have its steepness emphasized, just as Darcy's personal abruptness may be exaggerated, by the distance from which it is viewed.

Elizabeth's journey through the park, from its boundary to the house, is a spatial recapitulation of her association with Darcy from her first prejudiced impressions of his external appearance, through a recognition of other (and seemingly contradictory) views, to a final arrival at the central core of his character. As the reader follows Elizabeth's journey, he learns that although relativism and perspectivism are facts of existence—different people will see life from different windows, and movement through time and space inevitably provides different angles of view—variability is a function of human perception and not a characteristic of truth itself. That which is good and true in life resists the perversions of the individual viewpoint, as Pemberley is a beautiful scene from wherever it is viewed by Elizabeth.

Something of this Elizabeth had learned even before her visit to Darcy's estate; earlier, in a second discussion with Jane about Darcy's character, she had shown an awareness of the variability of the human viewpoint. Comparing Darcy to Wickham, she had once again refused to accede to Jane's indiscriminate benevolence, and had insisted (and here rightly) on a choice between the men: "There is but such a quantity of merit between them; just enough to make one good sort of man; and of late it has been shifting about pretty much. For my part, I am inclined to believe it all Mr. Darcy's but you shall do as you chuse." As Elizabeth's ironical tone implies, it is not the "merit" that has been shifting about, but the angle of view from which the two men have been judged. The merit is "all Mr. Darcy's," or as she later puts it, "One has got all the goodness, and the other all the appearance of it."

From the visit to Hunsford onward Elizabeth's vocabulary and the vocabulary of her reported thoughts take on something of Darcy's seriousness. If she had never entirely lacked judgment, her expressions now are studded with judicial phrases. As she "studie[s]" his letter, the "justice" of Darcy's charges becomes evident, and the "folly and indecorum of her own family" are brought home to her. Now, in a pivotal change of psychic direction, "her anger [is] turned against herself." Henceforth, her criticisms are frequently self-criticisms, or are directed inward on her family. She calls upon her father to "judge differently" in the affair of Lydia and the Brighton trip:

> It is not of peculiar, but of general evils, which I am now complaining. Our importance, our respectability in the world, must be affected by the wild volatility, the assurance and disdain of all restraint which mark Lydia's character. Excuse me—for I must speak plainly. If you, my dear father, will not take the trouble of . . . teaching her that her present pursuits are not to be the business of her life, she will soon be beyond the reach of amendment.

Her vocabulary adopts a Johnsonian tone[4] as she argues for general principles. She has moved from a personalist toward a social morality, and long before she is obliged to convince her father of her sincere love for Darcy, she has come to a recognition that "indeed he has no improper pride.". . .

A properly constituted society, Jane Austen insists, emerges only from the interaction of cultural discipline and individual commitment, and only when inherited forms receive the support of individual energy do they carry value. Conversely, however (and this is where Elizabeth's education is important), individual energy must be generated within social contexts, for, lacking social direction and control, it turns too easily to withdrawal from society, or to irresponsibility and anarchy. . . .

The best solution, clearly, is neither society alone, nor self alone, but self-in-society, the vitalized reconstitution of a social totality, the dynamic compromise between past and present, the simultaneous reception of what is valuable in an inheritance and the liberation of the originality, energy and spontaneity in the living moment. . . .

In a passage from the *Reflections* that I have used as an epigraph,[5] we may discover the thesis and antithesis of *Pride and Prejudice*. [Irish politician and writer Edmund] Burke

---

4. Samuel Johnson, a leading writer of the eighteenth century, was noted for his style.
5. "But in this, as in most questions of state, there is a middle. There is something else than the mere alternative of absolute destruction, or unreformed existence. . . . A disposition to preserve and an ability to improve, taken together, would be my standard of a statesman. Every thing else is vulgar in the conception, perilous in the execution."

requires as qualities of his ideal statesman a "disposition to preserve and an ability to improve," and it is exactly these requirements which are united in the marriage of Darcy and Elizabeth. Darcy's is the disposition to preserve, Elizabeth's the ability to improve, and taken together they achieve a synthesis which is not only (as Elizabeth recognizes) a "union . . . to the advantage of both" but a guarantee of a broader union in the fictional world of the novel.

Fate and Choice in *Pride and Prejudice*

C.C. Barfoot

C.C. Barfoot analyses the themes of fate and choice in *Pride and Prejudice*. Barfoot argues that for Austen choice is inevitable and necessary for liberty and independence but carries its own obligations. Fate, a word used only twice, is the enemy of choice and has no power over those who make the right choices for the right reasons. C.C. Barfoot has taught English at the University of Leiden in the Netherlands. He is the author of *The Clash of Ireland: Literary Contrasts and Connections* and *Theatre Intercontinental: Forms, Functions, Correspondences.*

Pride and Prejudice is the Jane Austen novel that turns its back most firmly on fate, whose existence it hardly cares to acknowledge, and consequently is most militant in its assertion of its belief in the virtue of choosing. Elizabeth Bennet says to Colonel Fitzwilliam of Darcy that he has 'great pleasure in the power of choice', adding with pointed criticism that she does 'not know any body who seems more to enjoy the power of doing what he likes than Mr. Darcy'. Elizabeth at this stage in their relationship suspects this power to choose, at least in the way it is exercised by Mr Darcy. Her blunt rejection of his unexpected, and not altogether flattering, proposal not long after these remarks, might be seen as an opportunity given her to confound Darcy's 'power of doing what he likes' that she is not able to resist. 'Liking' and 'not liking', 'why you like' or 'why you dislike', 'doing what you like' and 'not being able to do what you like' are the regular superficial ways in which people in *Pride and Prejudice,* as in other novels of Jane Austen's, touch upon and concern themselves with the business of making choices, and the intensely serious matter of making the right choices for the right reasons. . . .

Reprinted from C.C. Barfoot, *The Thread of Connection: Aspects of Fate in the Novels of Jane Austen and Others* (Amsterdam: Rodopi, 1982), by permission of the author.

One of the slightly unexpected elements of comedy in the novel derives from our realization that Darcy is no less moved by simple likes and dislikes than Lydia and Kitty, and indeed all the girls, are when gossiping and giggling over the young officers. But one of the things that he learns in the course of the novel is that many of one's choices are in fact prejudices and that even love is a kind of prejudice that can pre-empt one's rational choice, so that one finds oneself proposing to a girl despite her family. Similarly the girl herself learns that she can love and want to marry a man despite the initial response she provoked in him and enjoyed provoking and despite the fact that even at the end of the novel he has not yet learned 'to be laught at'. Paradoxically, *Pride and Prejudice* both demonstrates and asserts through comedy the importance of choice for the free spirit, yet at the same time irreverently considers the compulsions and the biases, the prejudices and the pressures that affect or hinder the finding and the selecting of the proper marriage partner. It is this complexity which ensures that *Pride and Prejudice* becomes more than a novel about the marriage market and the fluttering hearts and hopes of anxious young ladies, and vindicates the use of the traditional material of courtship and marriage as a means of dramatizing the issues of freedom and fate. . . .

CHOICE IS INEVITABLE AND REQUIRES RESPONSIBILITY

Pride and Prejudice makes it clear in small ways and in large that the responsibility of choice cannot be evaded. Mr Hurst thinks it 'rather singular' that Elizabeth prefers 'reading to cards'. But this is not merely a question of preferences either, for just after Mr Hurst's remark, Darcy caps Miss Bingley's account of a really accomplished woman with the demand that 'to all this she must add something more substantial, in the improvement of her mind by extensive reading'. Decisions about how to pass time in the drawing-room are all indications of the sensitivity of the individual to the responsibilities that are to be borne by the civilized man. Mary Bennet affirms, no doubt with the authority of her commonplace book, that 'society has claims on us all'; claims which for Darcy include the determination not to neglect the 'family library in such days as these'. . . .

It is inevitable that Pemberley should be responsible for so much of Darcy's gravity, since it represents the marvellous accretion of all the choices made by his predecessors, and has become 'a kind of model' for the way that the great power of choice that the possession of Pemberley entails should be discharged. This is felt both by the Bingleys, and by Elizabeth when she visits Pemberley with her aunt and uncle. It is there, on his home ground, that Darcy's basic civility, so lacking in his manner elsewhere, first displays itself. It is only then, trying to persuade Elizabeth that he is worthy of her and she of Pemberley and him, that he answers properly to his own inheritance. Just as Elizabeth tells Darcy that if she is not as good a pianist as she might have been, it is her own fault and not the fault of her fingers, since she 'would not take the trouble of practising'; so *Pride and Prejudice* as a whole reminds us continually that civilization is not a gift, perfect and complete, inherited by right or by chance, but is a possession that needs to be earned and sustained by practice; and one of the things it means is learning to catch the tone of the conversation of others and trying at least to appear 'interested in their concerns', for which Darcy, in the exchange that prompts Elizabeth's retort about piano-playing, admits his lack of talent. . . . After Darcy has replied to her invitation to admit his faults, Elizabeth agrees with him, 'you have chosen your fault well.—I really cannot *laugh* at it'.

RECURRENCE OF THE WORD "CHUSE"

On an earlier occasion, at Sir William Lucas's, Darcy had listened to Miss Bingley's malicious chatter 'with perfect indifference, while she chose to entertain herself in this manner'; while at the end of chapter IV, Bingley, gratified by his sister's praise of Jane Bennet's prettiness, 'felt authorised by such commendation to think of her as he chose'. Darcy objects to Bingley expecting him 'to account for opinions which you chuse to call mine'. Wickham says of Darcy that 'the world is blinded by his fortune and consequence, or frightened by his high and imposing manners, and sees him only as he chuses to be seen', and later grudgingly admits that 'Mr. Darcy can please where he chuses'. At the end of this same conversation Wickham pronounces that Darcy 'chuses that every one connected with him should have an understanding of the first class'. In the next chapter we are informed that 'the prospect of the Netherfield ball was extremely agreeable to every female of the [Bennet] family' and 'Mrs. Bennet chose to consider it as given in compliment to her eldest daughter'. When her mother suggests to Elizabeth that 'the probability' of her marriage with Mr Collins 'was exceedingly agreeable to *her*', we are told that 'Elizabeth however did not chuse to take the hint'.

However with so many choices laid before us while we read *Pride and Prejudice* and continually prompted to weigh the decisions of others by ourselves choosing who and what to believe, we can perhaps permit ourselves to take the hint and choose to see Mr Collins as the oracular emblem of the power of choice descending on the Bennet family. But it is as a parody of choice, since he is in fact an agent of fate, which in the guise of Lady Catherine de Bourgh has sent him forth with the august fiat to 'chuse properly, chuse a gentlewoman for *my* sake'. He makes no secret of the extent to which his independence and freedom are compromised, indeed he boasts of the way he is bound, and really he has no choice at all, either in choosing or in being chosen. As a clergyman, Mr Collins may be said to represent divine providence, for which his patroness is the mere earthly surrogate, and creditably he seeks 'a reconciliation with the Longbourne family', whose estate he is destined to inherit, and means 'to chuse one of the daughters, if he found them as handsome and amiable as they were represented by common report'. But truly Mr Collins is the very confusion of choice, with fate and destiny tucked in his clerical garb. . . .

'For this first evening Jane Bennet was his settled choice', but guided by Mrs Bennet, who hints that Jane is already chosen, he switches to Elizabeth, to whom he proposes with Old Testament fervour. Like a biblical patriarch, he tells her that in view of the fact that he is to inherit her father's estates he could not satisfy himself 'without resolving to chuse a wife from among his daughters'. Rejected by Elizabeth, he assures her, with self-gratifying condescension, that 'I shall chuse to attribute it to your wish of increasing my love by suspense'.

Austin's Use of the Words "Fate" and "Destiny"

It is not surprising that it is Mr Collins who uses the word 'fate' on one of the only two occasions it occurs in *Pride and Prejudice*. The first appearance of the word is not until chapter XVIII of the second volume, where we are told that 'the luckless Kitty continued in the parlour repining of her fate in terms as unreasonable as her accent was peevish'—her fate being, of course, not to be invited to Brighton. This is 'fate' used as part of the diction of spoilt and petulant young ladies, like Kitty and like Isabella Thorpe: a slangy usage which demeans an old philosophical notion, although in view of what happens to Lydia as consequence of her visit to the seaside, there is irony in Kitty using the word to express her annoyance at being precluded from sharing her sister's

---

FREQUENCY OF *FATE* IN AUSTEN'S NOVELS

Table 1 shows the frequency of the word fate *and related words in Austen's novels. Column 1 indicates the total number of words per occurrence of* fate, *column 2 the total number of words per occurrence of related words. For example,* fate *occurs once in every sixty-four thousand words in* Pride and Prejudice, *related words every sixteen thousand words. Table 2 shows the distribution of* fate *and specified related words in Austen's novels. (Both tables are based on sampling, not on computer count, and totals have been rounded to the nearest five hundred.)*

Table 1

	'fate'	related words
Northanger Abbey	25,000	11,000
Sense and Sensibility	15,500	15,000
Pride and Prejudice	64,000	16,000
Mansfield Park	16,000	8,500
Emma	25,000	10,000
Persuasion	17,000	8,000

Table 2

	'fate'	'destiny'	'lot'	'providence'	'fated'	'destined'	'fatal'	Total
NA	3	–	1	–	2[1]	–	1	7
SS	8	1	–	–	–	–	–	9
PP	2	–	2	–	–	4[2]	–	8
MP	10	2	4	1	1	1[3]	1	20
E	6	7	–	–	–	3	–	16
P	5	1	–	3	2[1]	–	1	12
Total	34	11	7	4	5	8	3	72

1. Includes 'ill-fated'.
2. Includes one 'self-destined'.
3. Includes one 'predestined'.

C.C. Barfoot, *The Thread of Connection: Aspects of Fate in the Novels of Jane Austen and Others*. Amsterdam: Rodopi, 1982.

adventures and, as it turns out, her fate.

But the word's next and last appearance is in the imposing context of Mr Collins's letter congratulating Mr Bennet on the engagement of one daughter to Bingley and hinting at the marriage of the second daughter whose 'chosen partner of her fate, may be reasonably looked up to, as one of the most illustrious personages in this land'. The notion of choosing the partner of one's fate is hackneyed, but still comes strangely from a clergyman who on his first visit to the Bennets 'protested that he never read novels': unwittingly it reveals the way in which for Mr Collins free choice is intertwined with and compromised by fate.

As one might expect, Mr Collins's noble patroness is the only other person in the novel who deigns to use such terms. Elizabeth has learned from Wickham that Darcy 'was evidently destined by Lady Catherine' to marry his cousin and unite the two estates. When Lady Catherine comes in person to change the course of family fortunes as they seem to be developing and put them back on the intended course, she first interrogatively, 'have you not heard me say, that from his earliest hours he was destined for his cousin?', and then with grand affirmation, 'they are destined for each other by the voice of every member of their respective houses', endorses the truth of Wickham's suggestion to the very letter. Lady Catherine challenges Elizabeth with 'what is to divide them?', which proves that the grand lady has not understood the implications of Elizabeth's earlier objection to the idea of destiny:

> 'If Mr. Darcy is neither by honour nor inclination confined to his cousin, why is not he to make another choice? And if I am that choice, why may not I accept him?'

This confrontation occurs before Darcy's second proposal which Elizabeth accepts. But it is her freedom from an engagement at this point that allows her, although neither indifferent to nor disinterested in the implications of Lady Catherine's visit and what it tells her of Darcy's probable intentions, and having now discovered that he is not as she had originally thought 'self-destined' to marry his cousin, to make the ringing declaration which lies at the heart of the concern in *Pride and Prejudice* with the power to choose:

> 'You are then resolved to have him?'
> 'I have said no such thing. I am only resolved to act in that manner, which will, in my opinion, constitute my happiness,

without reference to *you*, or to any person so wholly uncon-
nected with me.'

'It is well. You refuse, then, to oblige me. You refuse to obey
the claims of duty, honour, and gratitude. You are determined
to ruin him in the opinion of all his friends, and make him the
contempt of the world.'

'Neither duty, nor honour, nor gratitude,' replied Elizabeth, 'have any possible claim on me, in the present instance.
No principle of either, would be violated by my marriage with
Mr Darcy. And with regard to the resentment of his family, or
the indignation of the world, if the former *were* excited by his
marrying me, it would not give me one moment's concern—
and the world in general would have too much sense to join
in the scorn.'

Asked by her mother, after their visitor's abrupt departure,
'why Lady Catherine would not come in again and rest herself', Elizabeth can only reply, appropriately, 'she did not
choose it . . . she would go'. As far as *Pride and Prejudice* is
concerned, destiny, 'seriously displeased', has chosen, without taking her leave or sending compliments, in haste, to
quit the scene. . . .

OCCURRENCES OF CHANCE AND DESIGN

Chance, like fate and destiny, with which it is sometimes
identified, is the enemy of choice. Charlotte Lucas believes
that 'happiness in marriage is entirely a matter of chance'.
and proves it by accepting Mr Collins. Having captured her
man—and we can sympathize with her since at twenty-
seven she has reached a critical age in respect to her future
—Charlotte has the opportunity to test the advice that she
had earlier given Elizabeth about Jane: 'when she is secure
of him, there will be leisure for falling in love as much as she
chuses'. . . .

By her lack of faith in the value of choice, Charlotte plumps
entirely for chance, and makes both look like calculation or,
worse, like design. In *Pride and Prejudice* 'to have designs' is
to pose a threat to civility; and we can see why, since 'design'
may be conceived as a species of secular fate, a destiny engi-
neered by mortals to undermine and destroy the power of others to choose, an underhand attempt to make choice look like
chance or accident or to manipulate chance so that it is covered with the deceptive guise of choice. The word establishes
itself in a lightly ironic manner as one of the true antitheses of
choice in the first chapter when, following Mrs Bennet's assertion that she is thinking of Bingley marrying one of her

daughters, Mr Bennet asks 'is this his design in settling here?';
while five chapters later, in a conversation with Charlotte
Elizabeth denies that Jane is 'acting by design' with respect to
her feelings for Bingley. This is subsequently followed by
more insidious implications in the way the word is used, so
that on occasions 'design' comes very close to connoting in-
tentional evil. In a more comic vein, but with his usual dead-
ening air of self-congratulation that is here especially chilling,
Mr Collins announces that he and Charlotte 'seem to be designed for each other'. Mr Collins is, as always, blithely unconscious of what his words reveal and as confused as his noble patroness, who in her matrimonial plans mistakes design
for destiny.

But those with the most serious designs in *Pride and Prejudice* are Miss Bingley and Wickham, who we feel really are
designed for each other as fellow predators, but here destiny
like their designs goes astray and they are both pushed to the
side of the stage. Wickham as a designer of charm gets more
credit and greater rewards than Miss Bingley, who, however,
thinks 'it advisable to retain the right of visiting Pemberley',
where on her visits she pays 'off every arrear of civility to
Elizabeth' and no doubt continues to seek opportunities to
display her figure to advantage.

With supreme comic confidence *Pride and Prejudice* asserts
that neither fate nor chance has power over men who have the
right kind of pride and are determined to maintain their freedom to choose; nor is calculation or design able to exploit the
prejudices of those who can be educated through love to learn
to make the discriminations necessary for the responsible exercise of choice. This optimism, reflected in the *brio*[1] of the
novel, accounts for its unceasing popularity and establishes it
as a work that we should not ignore in our reflections about
the nature and conditions of independence and liberty.

1. vigor; vivacity

CHAPTER 2

Characters

READINGS ON
PRIDE AND PREJUDICE

Elizabeth's Teasing Charms Darcy

John Hardy

John Hardy analyzes Elizabeth's early conversations with Darcy to show his fascination with her intelligence and wit, even as she uses both to insult him. Endowed with a blend of sweetness and playfulness, Elizabeth teases in ways that penetrate Darcy's pretentions and eventually cause him to change, according to Hardy, who also argues that Elizabeth's teasing fosters intimacy and sexuality in their relationship and infuses it with delight. John Hardy, scholar of seventeenth- and eighteenth-century literature, is the author of *Reinterpretations: Essays on Poems by Milton, Pope, and Johnson* and editor of *The Political Writings of Dr. Johnson: A Selection.*

Pride and Prejudice contains the most famous opening sentence in English literature: 'It is a truth universally acknowledged, that a single man in possession of a good fortune, must be in want of a wife'. At the same time, no two characters would, on the face of it, seem less likely to marry than Elizabeth Bennet and Fitzwilliam Darcy. Because of his manner of slighting her at the ball, she has from the start 'no very cordial feelings towards him'; and so overwhelming is her initial 'prejudice' because of his seemingly repulsive 'pride', that the reader wonders by what process they could ever come together. Yet they do almost immediately notice each other; and that he can afterwards bring himself to propose to her indicates that something important has been passing between them—something sufficient, in itself, to begin to humanise Darcy. . . .

Though he at first observes her critically, noticing that she has 'hardly a good feature in her face', he soon finds it 'rendered uncommonly intelligent by the beautiful expres-

From *Jane Austen's Heroines: Intimacy in Human Relationships*, by John Hardy (London: Routledge & Kegan Paul, 1984). Reprinted by permission of the publisher.

sion of her dark eyes' and is 'caught' by the 'easy playfulness' of her 'manners'. While these are 'not those of the fashionable world', Darcy is bound to redefine the conventional view of female 'accomplishments' by what so interests him in Elizabeth. When her friend Charlotte Lucas insists that she 'play and sing' to the assembled company, it is not Elizabeth's 'performance' that captivates Darcy; instead it is the liveliness with which she seeks to confirm his dislike. She has mentioned to Charlotte why she has to exert herself against him, and soon has the opportunity of suiting her action to her words. On Darcy's approaching them 'though without seeming to have any intention of speaking', Elizabeth is provoked to address him:

> 'Did not you think, Mr. Darcy, that I expressed myself uncommonly well just now, when I was teazing Colonel Forster to give us a ball at Meryton?'
> 'With great energy;—but it is a subject which always makes a lady energetic.'
> 'You are severe on us.'
> 'It will be *her* turn soon to be teazed,' said Miss Lucas. 'I am going to open the instrument, Eliza, and you know what follows.'

The 'teasing' here works against Elizabeth not Darcy: Charlotte presses her to play, and Elizabeth's verbal display merely gives him the opportunity of turning her words to her seeming disadvantage. In future conversations, however, she does not so easily lose the advantage. Indeed, as she makes Darcy's words and manner the target of her wit, she forces him to modify both his own preconceptions and the air of aloof superiority he has too easily arrogated to himself. Her teasing of him becomes, in fact, the essence of her own 'performance' and the means of interesting him so thoroughly instead of (as she supposes) driving him away.

This becomes obvious during Elizabeth's first evening at Netherfield, when Miss Bingley seeks to ingratiate herself with Darcy by praising his sister Georgiana. There is, however, nothing in Miss Bingley's manner to animate Darcy, who comments as follows on the conventional list of female accomplishments mentioned by her brother:

> 'Your list of the common extent of accomplishments,' said Darcy, 'has too much truth. The word is applied to many a woman who deserves it no otherwise than by netting a purse, or covering a skreen. But I am very far from agreeing with you in your estimation of ladies in general. I cannot boast of

knowing more than half a dozen, in the whole range of my acquaintance, that are really accomplished.'

'Nor I, I am sure,' said Miss Bingley.

Yet Darcy's proves an extreme view, extreme because apparently unrealistic, and Elizabeth is prompted to tackle him about it:

'Then,' observed Elizabeth, 'you must comprehend a great deal in your idea of an accomplished woman.'

'Yes; I do comprehend a great deal in it.'

'Oh! certainly,' cried his faithful assistant, 'no one can be really esteemed accomplished, who does not greatly surpass what is usually met with. A woman must have a thorough knowledge of music, singing, drawing, dancing, and the modern languages, to deserve the word; and besides all this, she must possess a certain something in her air and manner of walking, the tone of her voice, her address and expressions, or the word will be but half deserved.'

'All this she must possess,' added Darcy, 'and to all this she must yet add something more substantial, in the improvement of her mind by extensive reading.'

'I am no longer surprised at your knowing *only* six accomplished women. I rather wonder now at your knowing *any.*'

'Are you so severe upon your own sex, as to doubt the possibility of all this?'

'*I* never saw such a woman. *I* never saw such capacity, and taste, and application, and elegance, as you describe, united.'

. . . The relationship of Elizabeth and Darcy begins in a haughty aloofness on his side and a readiness to oppose him on hers; yet her constant challenging of him fosters and holds his interest. . . .

Darcy comes to respond not merely to Elizabeth's 'fine eyes' but to her fine intelligence, and one senses in their conversations at Netherfield, and later at Rosings, how much he welcomes her stimulating presence. When her mother visits Jane at Netherfield and displays to the company her fussy self-importance and shameless want of understanding, Elizabeth takes the conversation on to another plane and has Darcy smile at her wit in opposing the notion that poetry is 'the food of love'. Indeed, her stimulating presence becomes infinitely more interesting to him than merely conventional pleasures. When, having finished a letter, he asks 'for the indulgence of some music', he takes the opportunity of 'a lively Scotch air' for 'drawing near' her and asking whether she feels like dancing. At this he receives a spirited rebuff. Elizabeth had 'rather expected to affront him . . . but there was a mixture of sweetness and archness[1] in her manner which made it difficult for her to affront anybody', and Darcy, it is said, 'had never been so bewitched by any woman as he was by her'.

ELIZABETH ELEVATES HER TEASING

During their final conversation at Netherfield, many of the points that have already begun to emerge are subtly reinforced and extended; and a further important point is introduced—the implicit connection between intimacy and teasing. Miss Bingley, despite her assertion of that 'certain something' a woman should 'possess', fails to attract Darcy's attention by walking 'about the room', and only succeeds in doing so after she has invited Elizabeth to join her. Yet because of her wheedling coyness she leaves Elizabeth and herself open to hearing Darcy's reasons for not joining them. '"Oh! shocking!" cried Miss Bingley. "I never heard any thing so abominable. How shall we punish him for such a speech?"' Elizabeth suggests they should 'teaze him—laugh at him', adding: 'Intimate as you are, you must know how it is to be done.' Miss Bingley, however, who lacks the wit to express herself towards Darcy in such a manner, considers this impossible.

> 'Mr. Darcy is not to be laughed at!' cried Elizabeth. 'That is an uncommon advantage, and uncommon I hope it will continue, for it would be a great loss to *me* to have many such acquaintance. I dearly love a laugh.'
>
> 'Miss Bingley,' said he, 'has given me credit for more than can be. The wisest and the best of men, nay, the wisest and best of their actions, may be rendered ridiculous by a person whose first object in life is a joke.' 'Certainly,' replied Elizabeth—'there are such people, but I hope I am not one of *them*. I hope I never ridicule what is wise or good. Follies and nonsense, whims and inconsistencies *do* divert me, I own, and I laugh at them whenever I can.—But these, I suppose, are precisely what you are without.'
>
> 'Perhaps that is not possible for any one. But it has been the study of my life to avoid those weaknesses which often expose a strong understanding to ridicule.'
>
> 'Such as vanity and pride.'
>
> 'Yes, vanity is a weakness indeed. But pride—where there is a real superiority of mind, pride will be always under good regulation.'
>
> Elizabeth turned away to hide a smile.

1. mischievousness; playfulness

'Your examination of Mr. Darcy is over, I presume,' said Miss Bingley;—and pray what is the result?'

'I am perfectly convinced by it that Mr. Darcy has no defect. He owns it himself without disguise.'

Elizabeth has, in fact, teased Darcy in a way that reminds us of the derivation of the word. Her words act like a teasel: intended to be pricking to a far greater degree than merely pin-pricking, they tease out and raise the nap on his character. And obviously he finds this both unusual and stimulating. Though it calls forth some seriousness on his part, he is also committed to responding, and may even be felt to do so with a trace of eagerness:

'No'—said Darcy, 'I have made no such pretension. I have faults enough, but they are not, I hope, of understanding. My temper I dare not vouch for.—It is I believe too little yielding— certainly too little for the convenience of the world. I cannot forget the follies and vices of others so soon as I ought, nor their offences against myself. My feelings are not puffed about with every attempt to move them. My temper would perhaps be called resentful.—My good opinion once lost is lost for ever.'

'*That* is a failing indeed!'—cried Elizabeth. 'Implacable resentment *is* a shade in a character. But you have chosen your fault well.—I really cannot *laugh* at it. You are safe from me.'

'There is, I believe, in every disposition a tendency to some particular evil, a natural defect, which not even the best education can overcome.'

'And *your* defect is a propensity to hate every body.'

'And yours,' he replied with a smile, 'is wilfully to misunderstand them.'

ELIZABETH'S TEASING EVOKES INTIMACY

Elizabeth and Darcy have between them a conversation to which the music Miss Bingley then calls for becomes merely a safe and lesser alternative. Though his friend Bingley has previously tried to answer him by remarks more nearly personal—as when he pictures him as a most 'aweful object' at home of a Sunday evening—Elizabeth's spirited rallying of Darcy, accompanied, as it is, by 'a mixture of sweetness and archness in her manner', not merely excites his interest but has the potential for establishing something more like intimacy between them. Even though she later admits to him to never having spoken 'without rather wishing to give [him] pain than not', her words prevent Darcy from taking refuge in arrogance and force him to engage with real questions about himself. They pursue him closely in a manner in which he is willing to be pursued. Again they prompt him to 'smile', which is an indication not so much of his satisfaction at what he has said as of his interest in Elizabeth and in what, above all, has aroused this—the play of wit and intelligence which marks her personality and which he has the discrimination and intelligence to appreciate and respond to. Despite the pride and prejudice on each side, which for so long keep them apart, their conversations together have what only they can share. Elizabeth's lively and challenging remarks arouse his interest in a special way; and in demanding an immediate return, they put him on his mettle. . . .

TEASING REAPPEARS WITH RESPECT

While the novel is something of a *tour de force*,[2] in seeking to metamorphose Darcy's 'pride' from something repulsive to something we can almost forgive, our sense of what Elizabeth and Darcy will eventually share is not based merely on the altered feelings that each displays on meeting again in Derbyshire. Though Elizabeth's 'deeper sentiment of gratitude' at Darcy's 'regard' is increased by his efforts to preserve Lydia's social respectability in having Wickham marry her, what has earlier passed between them reappears with a new sparkle towards the end of the novel.

When, however, Darcy comes to Longbourn, Elizabeth has some distressing moments. She is 'astonished and vexed' when he sits silent and reserved, saying to herself, 'If he no longer cares for me, why silent? Teazing, teazing, man! I will think no more about him'. Of course, Darcy is not deliberately setting out to tease Elizabeth: as he later explains, he was 'embarrassed' and, given the strength of his feelings for her, unable to converse with ease; but because of what Elizabeth has come to feel for him, his silence is teasing in the extreme. It presents the kind of challenge which she cannot get the better of, much as her own conversation had done to Darcy. Later, when all is settled between them, though her attitude to Darcy has long since changed, her latent challenging of him continues to draw them together. Even in the post-mortem they hold on earlier feelings and events, though each has a need to be—and even enjoys being—serious and self-critical, there is often a liveliness in Elizabeth's words that is just below the surface.

2. a task requiring great virtuosity, often deliberately undertaken for its difficulty

A hint of this can be seen in her response to Darcy's hope that she does not have 'the power' of reading again the opening of his letter: 'The letter shall certainly be burnt, if you believe it essential to the preservation of my regard'. When Darcy has explained to her why he was so 'grave and silent' on meeting her again, Elizabeth replies, 'How unlucky that you should have a reasonable answer to give, and that I should be so reasonable as to admit it'. Such a remark proves that she is in no danger of making the kind of 'unequal marriage' which her father at first fears she might make in marrying someone she cannot 'respect', for Elizabeth would be unable to respond to a man in this way unless she both respected his intelligence and felt confident of his appreciation in return. Such good-humoured teasing is meant to be pleasantly provoking, and to this extent is in fact covertly sexual. . . .

The very thing that attracts Darcy to Elizabeth is what gives the lie to the suggestion that she needs to abandon her individual 'consciousness' in order to find happiness with him. When she rather provokingly asks, 'Did you admire me for my impertinence?', he aptly replies, 'For the liveliness of your mind, I did.' Conventional 'accomplishments', whether as a means of defence or allurement, form no part of her make-up or intentions. Instead she expresses her quintessential self in her conversational exchanges with him. One striking example of the playfulness of her wit occurs when she herself makes this very point:

> 'You were disgusted with the women who were always speaking and looking, and thinking for *your* approbation alone. I roused, and interested you, because I was so unlike *them.* Had you not been really amiable you would have hated me for it; but in spite of the pains you took to disguise yourself, your feelings were always noble and just; and in your heart, you thoroughly despised the persons who so assiduously courted you. There—I have saved you the trouble of accounting for it; and really, all things considered, I begin to think it perfectly reasonable. To be sure, you knew no actual good of me—but nobody thinks of *that* when they fall in love.'

Here Elizabeth gives even Darcy's earlier behaviour a handsome and affectionate gloss, without giving up, moreover, the delight of still teasing him. By her behaviour she fashions him into a fitting companion for herself, for Darcy has the discrimination and responsiveness to rise to the challenge. Obviously he will continue to find her as bewitching and fascinating as he ever did.

Elizabeth's and Darcy's Mutual Mortification and Renewal

Stuart M. Tave

According to Stuart M. Tave, mortification, or humiliation, changes Elizabeth and Darcy, making their
happy marriage possible. Tave gives examples of the
couple's painful experiences that lead to humiliation.
In particular, two events lead to changing attitudes:
Darcy's letter following his proposal, and Lydia's
elopement. Stuart M. Tave has been professor of English at the University of Chicago. He is the author of
*The Amiable Humorist: A Study in the Comic Theory
and Criticism of Eighteenth and Early Nineteenth
Centuries* and *New Essays by De Quincey.*

The first time Elizabeth Bennet sees Mr. Darcy, before they
have ever spoken to each other, he mortifies her. It is the beginning of their action. His character has been decided already, by all the principal people in the room; Bingley has
such amiable qualities as must speak for themselves, but—
what a contrast between him and his friend!—Darcy is the
proudest, most disagreeable man in the world. Before the
action ends Elizabeth will have to discover that this is a
really amiable man, to whom she must give her affection.
She will have to define the differences between the agreeable and the amiable and to define the foundations of affection; and he will have to become worthy of that process of
painful definition. It will be a mortifying experience for both
of them. . . .

When, at last, [Darcy] can tell [Elizabeth] of his feelings,
they prove how important she has been to him, and they
make "his affection every moment more valuable." That is
what enables her to answer her father's doubts of Darcy
with "absolute certainty that his affection was not the work

of a day, but had stood the test of many months suspense." She is "in the certain possession of his warmest affection."

They have come to that happy moment because each has suffered a change. If he has no improper pride and is perfectly amiable when she accepts him, he was not so when she rejected him. And if she is capable of the kind of affection she feels when she accepts him, she was not so when she rejected him. Each has changed because each has worked a change on the other. The happiness is deserved by a process of mortification begun early and ended late. Charlotte Lucas suggested at the start that Darcy is a man who has some right to be proud, and Elizabeth agrees. I could easily forgive *his* pride, if he had not mortified *mine*." As Mary Bennet, on the same page, draws upon her reading of synonym dictionaries to define pride, we can get some help from these sources in understanding mortification. It is more than the mere vexation of a contradictory will, it is a force that cuts into the understanding and evaluation of one's self. Mrs. Bennet is easily vexed—"You take delight in vexing me," she says in the first chapter. "You have no compassion on my poor nerves"—but she cannot be mortified. Elizabeth will have to make the distinction. Vexation arises from the crossing our wishes and views, says Crabb's *English Synonymes* (1816), "*mortification* from the hurting our pride and self-importance.". . .

STAGES IN ELIZABETH'S AND DARCY'S RELATIONSHIP

Mortification, in Jane Austen's language, no longer has a religious force. . . . But it can be, we know, much stronger than a social term for an embarrassment; it can still carry a moral, renovative, force. Elizabeth and Darcy change one another because each hurts the pride and self-importance of the other, humbling, humiliating, forcing a self-recognition that requires a giving up of part of the character for which each has always felt self-esteem and a taking on of a new character. That each is capable of the loss and the renewal by mortification is what makes the love valuable. The inception, the turning point, and then the resolution of the changing relationship of Elizabeth and Darcy are, each of them, marked by mortifications: the first rousing effect each has on the other; the unsuccessful proposal and the letter that follows; and the elopement of Lydia, the event necessary for a fitting successful proposal. Each signalizes a challenge that calls forth a revealing response either of self-protective failure or of self-conquest.

The process begins immediately upon the first occasion of their being together, when Darcy looks for a moment at Elizabeth, till catching her eye, then withdraws his own and coldly refuses to dance with her because she is not handsome enough to tempt "*me*": Elizabeth could easily forgive *his* pride, "if he had not mortified *mine*." Without his intending it, and without her knowing it, he has indicated the sort of lesson Elizabeth must learn. Pride relates to our opinion of ourselves, Mary Bennet says, and it is that pride which now begins to be and will be more properly and more severely mortified. It is he, however, his withdrawn eye, which is most in need of education at this point, and the very next thing we hear of him is that she becomes an object of some interest in his eye; having scarcely allowed her to be pretty and looking at her, when they meet again, only to criticize, and making clear to himself and his friends that she has hardly a good feature in her face, he then finds the intelligence and beauty of her eyes. "To this discovery succeeded some others equally mortifying." Though he has detected with critical eye more than one failure in the perfect symmetry of her form, he is now forced to acknowledge that it is light and pleasing; though he has asserted that her manners are not fashionable he is now caught by their easy playfulness. The return upon himself is just, as she, unknowingly, is catching and forcing him to admit that he has been mistaken. The first important effect each has on the other is a mortification, a lowering of self-opinion. But neither has yet been able to benefit from the effect; the effect has not been strong enough, in good part because neither is in a moral position to make the other feel the effect.

The turning point of their developing relation is Darcy's proposal to Elizabeth and his rejection. He has no right to propose. Elizabeth is quite right to reject him; he would not be a good husband. He has not, even in proposing, behaved in a gentlemanlike manner and is startled to told that truth, and more than startled: "You could not have made me the offer of your hand in any possible way that would have tempted me to accept it"; this he must hear from the woman whose pride he mortified by saying she was not handsome enough to tempt *him*. He looks at her with "mingled incredulity and mortification." She goes on and begins to re-

move the incredulity by describing how from the first moment of their acquaintance his deficiencies of manner impressed her with that fullest belief in his arrogance, conceit,
and selfish disdain of the feelings of others that formed the
groundwork on which succeeding events have built so im-
movable a dislike. Her accusations are ill founded, formed
on mistaken premises, but, as he later says, his behavior to
her merited the severest reproach and the mortification remains. It is from this point that Darcy's life changes importantly. It takes time. The recollection of what he said, his
conduct, his manners, his expression, is for many months
inexpressibly painful. Her reproof, that he had not behaved
in a gentlemanlike manner—the words remain with him—
had been a torture, and it was some time before he was reasonable enough to allow their justice. To a man of principle
the pain of realizing the pride and selfishness of a lifetime is
a hard lesson and he owes much to her who taught him. "By
you, I was properly humbled."

What we see of Darcy, of course, is mainly the result of
what has happened, not the many months of pain; we see
him through Elizabeth's eyes and share with her the surprise of what has happened and understand it in retrospect
as it moves her. As Elizabeth rejects Darcy, producing the
mortification that changes his life, our interest, as always, is
in what will happen to her, and what happens to her,
painfully and fortunately, is the letter from him producing
the mortification that changes her life. It comes as a particularly powerful blow to her because it makes her know the
meaning of feelings she has experienced repeatedly and
never understood; the causes of mortification have been at
work and she has felt them without recognizing their import. They have been at work in what is closest to her, in her
own family, in her friend, in the man she has found so
agreeable, in herself.

ELIZABETH'S BLIND CONFIDENCE

Elizabeth has always been confident in knowing the truth,
immediately and exactly. She has believed the history of
himself that Wickham gave: there was truth in his looks.
Jane finds it difficult to decide between the conflicting accounts she has heard—it is distressing—one does not know
what to think. But Elizabeth knows: "I beg your pardon;—
one knows exactly what to think." It is the certainty that car-

ries her straight to that extraordinary carnival of foolishness, so wealthy in detail, the Netherfield ball. She dances
herself into what is, exactly, a dance of mortification, totally
misunderstood by her. The prospect of that ball, extremely
agreeable to every female of her family, brings to Elizabeth
the pleasurable thought of dancing a great deal with Wickham and seeing a confirmation of everything in Darcy's
looks and behavior. Her spirits are so high that they carry
her away and though she does not often speak unnecessar-
ily to Mr. Collins she cannot help asking whether he is going
and whether he will think it proper to join the amusement.
To her surprise he is not only prepared to dance but takes
the opportunity she has offered by securing her for the first
two dances. She feels herself completely taken in, is her own
victim. She had fully proposed being engaged by Wickham
for those very dances—and to have Mr. Collins instead! her
liveliness had never been worse timed. She enters the dancing room at Netherfield to look for Wickham, a doubt of his
being present having never occurred to her, certain of meeting him, dressed with more than usual care and prepared in
the highest spirits for completing the conquest that evening.
But he is not there. She suspects that it is Darcy who has
caused his exclusion, then finds that it is Wickham who has
wished to avoid Darcy and is thereby assured that Darcy is
no less answerable for Wickham's absence than if her first
surmise had been just. Pursuing that line of justice in her
disappointment she is hardly able to reply with tolerable civility to Darcy's politeness, because attention, forbearance,
or patience with him is injury to Wickham, and she turns
from him in ill humor. She turns to Charlotte Lucas, tells
that friend all her griefs, makes a voluntary transition to the
oddities of her cousin Collins, whom Charlotte has not yet
seen, and points him out to the particular notice of her
friend. Charlotte takes particular notice.

DISAGREEABLE DANCES AT THE NETHERFIELD BALL

Three sets of dances follow. The first dances are with Mr.
Collins and bring distress, as in his awkwardness and solem-
nity and often moving wrong without being aware of it he
gives her all the shame and misery a disagreeable partner can
give: they are "dances of mortification." The moment of re-
lease from him is ecstasy. Wickham is not there but she next
dances with a fellow officer of his and has the refreshment of

talking of Wickham and hearing that he is universally liked. Then she finds herself suddenly addressed by Darcy, "who took her so much by surprise in his application for her hand, that, without knowing what she did, she accepted him." She is then left to fret over her presence of mind while Charlotte tries to console her by saying she will find him very agreeable. That is the succession of her partners, of the three men who will be, or seem to be, solicitous of her hand and who present to her problems of increasing complexity. She delivers herself into the hands of each with an increasing ironic ignorance, finally accepting Darcy in spite of her determination to hate that disagreeable man. Darcy had once rejected her as a partner, mortifying *her* (italicized) pride. It was her mother's advice then that at another time she should not dance with *him* and Elizabeth believed she could safely promise *never* to dance with him. It was a promise she kept, when the opportunity first offered, at Sir William Lucas's; her resistance to Darcy did not injure her with the gentleman. Now, at Netherfield, she accepts him and is unhappy she has lost that assured control of a mind which, a few pages before, knows exactly what to think. We never hear of her dancing with anyone else after that, but it will be a while before she will understand the meaning of what she has done. She dances badly, in fact, taking the occasion not to learn more of Darcy's mind and character but, in a sudden fancy, to punish him. She is unable to resist the temptation of forcing the subject of Wickham on him, even blaming herself for weakness in not going on with it more than she does. There are times when she literally does not know what she is saying because her mind is wandering to Wickham and she then asks searching questions of Darcy's character that are more immediately relevant to her own blindness. Elizabeth is perfectly satisfied that she knows his character and Wickham's, and contradictory information that evening, whether from Miss Bingley or from Jane, can only confirm her; she is acutely analytic in refusing to accept what they say, and she is wholly mistaken in her conclusion. Changing the subject then to Jane's modest hopes of Bingley's regard, Elizabeth, always confident, says all in her power to heighten Jane's confidence.

THE BENNETS EMBARRASS ELIZABETH

Perfectly satisfied with herself she is forced by the conduct of her family into a series of confused vexations and morti-

fications. Mr. Collins discovers wonderfully that Mr. Darcy is
a nephew of Lady Catherine, insists on introducing himself,
and though Elizabeth tries hard to dissuade him, determines
to follow his own inclination; it "vexed" her to see him expose himself to such a man. She is then deeply "vexed" to
find that her mother is talking openly of her expectation of
Jane's marriage to Bingley; Elizabeth tries to check Mrs.
Bennet or make her less audible, for to her "inexpressible
vexation" she perceives that Darcy is overhearing; but nothing she says has any influence: "Elizabeth blushed and
blushed again with shame and vexation." With a brief inter-
val of tranquillity she then has the "mortification" of seeing
Mary oblige the company by exhibiting herself in a song.
Elizabeth suffers most painful sensations and agonies, until
at her look of entreaty her father interferes, in a speech that
makes her still more sorry. Mr. Collins takes the opportunity
to make a worse fool of himself before Darcy, which amuses
Mr. Bennet and draws a serious commendation from Mrs.
Bennet. To Elizabeth it appears that had the family made an
agreement to expose themselves as much as possible they
could not have played their parts with finer success; and all
she misses is her own even finer part. The greatest relief in
all this she owes to her friend Charlotte, who often good-
naturedly engages Mr. Collins's conversation to herself.
Darcy never comes near enough to speak again and feeling
it to be the probable consequence of her allusions to Wickham Elizabeth rejoices in it. It has been an evening of wonderfully compounded errors. Mrs. Bennet, like Elizabeth, is
"perfectly satisfied."

FURTHER MORTIFICATION FOLLOWS OVERCONFIDENCE

But from that point of satisfaction the series of vexations and
mortifications, unprofitable because misunderstood, begins
to work upon her. Mr. Collins's proposal the next day is vexing and embarrassing, but Elizabeth can overcome that
problem; the private acknowledgment of Wickham, that his
regret and vexation at having been absent was in fact a self-
imposed necessity to avoid Darcy, meets with her approval;
the possibility, in Bingley's sudden and unexpected departure, that he may never return to Jane, she treats with contempt. The first serious surprise to her is the revelation that
Charlotte's continued kindness in keeping Mr. Collins in
good humor, for which Elizabeth is more obliged than she

can express, is a kindness that extends further than Elizabeth has any conception of. Elizabeth could not have supposed it possible that her friend could have sacrificed every better feeling to worldly advantage. "Charlotte the wife of Mr. Collins, was a most humiliating picture!" The humiliation is hers. It then becomes clear that Bingley will not return and that Jane's hope is entirely over. The perfectly satisfied Elizabeth finds herself becoming dissatisfied, not with herself but with the world; every day confirms her belief of the inconsistency of all human characters and of the little dependence that can be placed on the appearance of either merit or sense; Bingley is one instance and Charlotte is the other. Nor will she allow Jane to defend Charlotte or for the sake of one individual change the meaning of principle and integrity, confuse selfishness with prudence. Finally the sole survivor of her apparent satisfactions at the Netherfield ball disappears, as Wickham's apparent partiality subsides and he becomes the admirer of someone else, someone whose most remarkable charm is the sudden acquisition of ten thousand pounds. But Elizabeth, so dissatisfied with the inconsistency of human character, less clear-sighted in this case than in Charlotte's, finds his wish of independence entirely natural. If she did not think so, if she did not think she would be his only choice if fortune permitted, that fortune denied him by that abominable Mr. Darcy, she would be forced to think differently of herself. She is not young in the ways of the world, she says, and she is "open to the mortifying conviction" that handsome young men must have something to live on. In her subsequent conversation about Wickham, with Mrs. Gardiner, she seems to have lost sight of the difference in matrimonial affairs between the mercenary and the prudent motive, a difference so clear to her in Charlotte's affair. Then follows a series of observations concluding in the exclamation that she is sick of all men, that she is thankful to be visiting the home of Mr. Collins in Kent, because he has not one agreeable quality, because stupid men are the only ones worth knowing after all. Mrs. Gardiner's warning to take care, that her speech savors strongly of disappointment, is serious. The vexations and the mortifications, with their separate meanings, have all collapsed into one, into a disappointed condemnation of others for their contradictory conduct to her. Because she cannot turn them to an occasion of growth they begin to harm her.

ELIZABETH MORTIFIES DARCY; HIS LETTER MORTIFIES HER

The turning point is in her visit to Kent, not because she meets again a stupid and disagreeable man but because she meets Darcy again. She mortifies him, in what is his most valuable moment, but not hers; she does it in the blindness and prejudice of the mind she has brought to Kent. Her moment follows when she receives, in return, his letter revealing to her what she must know to convert her own badly understood mortifications into a real mortification. Her feelings are acutely painful, difficult of definition. Her first reaction is to disbelieve what he says, it must be false, it cannot be true, because if it is true it will overthrow every cherished opinion, and she puts the letter away hastily, protesting she will not regard it, never look at it again. The value of Elizabeth is that this will not do, the pain and the difficulty must be borne, and in half a minute, collecting herself as well as she could, "she again began the mortifying perusal of all that related to Wickham," commanding herself to examine the meaning of every sentence. It is the necessary first step in the understanding of the real character of Wickham and of herself; the result is the eye-opening moment, as she grows absolutely ashamed of herself, her actions, her pride in her own discernment and her disdain of others. "How humiliating is this discovery!—Yet, how just a humiliation!" It is the mortification of self-discovery. "Till this moment, I never knew myself." From this knowledge it follows that when she returns once more to the letter, to that part of it in which her family are mentioned "in terms of such mortifying, yet merited reproach," her sense of shame is severe, especially when she remembers the Netherfield ball. She knows now the justice of those terms.

There is a new self-knowledge in Elizabeth. It is evident, in a minor way, in her return to Hertfordshire, when she hears Lydia describe the girl to whom Wickham had transferred his admiration; such a nasty little freckled thing, Lydia calls her, and Elizabeth is shocked to think that if she is incapable of such coarseness of expression herself, the coarseness of sentiment is what her own breast had formerly harbored and fancied liberal. She and Darcy have given severe lessons of liberality to each other and each is in a proper course to make use of what has been learned. What is needed is an incident that will put them to the test of action. It is a sad moment for Kitty when Lydia receives her invitation to Brighton: the rapture of Lydia, the delight of Mrs. Bennet and the mortification of Kitty are scarcely to be described; but in that company it is obvious that the effect on Kitty is not improving, and worse must follow if any good is to result to her. It comes through the more serious mortification of others when Lydia runs off with Wickham. The incident may be of excessive length and fuss for the balance of the novel, but it is a necessary weight for the two main characters, who must now bear the effects of their past, the old self, and respond with the liberal conquest of the new self. The alteration in Darcy's and in Elizabeth's understanding, consequent upon their mutual mortifications, has been large; but it is Lydia's elopement that brings the concluding mortifications and the deserved happiness.

LYDIA'S ELOPEMENT: THE FINAL MORTIFICATION AND SUBSEQUENT HAPPINESS

To Elizabeth the elopement is "humiliation" and misery. It justifies Darcy in the two chief causes of offense she had laid to his charge—his offenses against Wickham and against her family—and it brings those two forces together in such a way as to sink Elizabeth's power over him. She believes that he has now made a self-conquest, is no longer subject to his feelings for her, and the belief is exactly calculated to make her understand her own wishes, that she could have loved him. Later, after Lydia's marriage is assured, Elizabeth is heartily sorry that in her distress of the moment she had told Darcy of her fears for Lydia; the beginning could have been concealed from him: there was no one whose knowledge of her sister's frailty could have "mortified her so much." But it is not from any hope for herself, because the gulf between her and Darcy is now impassable, both her objectionable family and Wickham. She is wrong, but now it is to her credit. She accepts her loss. Even when she has learned what Darcy has in fact done she must hide her feelings: it was necessary to laugh when she would rather have cried; her father had most cruelly mortified her by what he said of Mr. Darcy's indifference to her. Her father may be right.

What she did not know, and her ignorance is no fault in her, is that Darcy is stronger than she could have thought. He has made a self-conquest more difficult than the one she

imagined, by taking responsibility for Wickham's act, by ex-
erting himself, by going to Wickham and arranging the marriage. It was "an exertion of goodness" she had thought too
great to be probable, but it was not: "he had taken on himself all the trouble and mortification" of searching out and
supplicating and bribing those he had most reason to abom-
inate, despise, avoid. He had done it, though she still cannot
realize that fully, because of "his affection for her." When
she finally has the opportunity she thanks him for the compassion that enabled him to take so much trouble and "bear
so many mortifications." And, rightly, it is then that she
learns it was done not for her family but for her, and she
knows the value of his affection. Their story comes to a
happy ending earned by two properly humbled people who
have learned to bear mortification and to rise under it with
love.

There are deserved little rewards at the end in the re-
moval of mortifications, when Elizabeth and Darcy can
leave the mortifying society of her family, when even Mary
Bennet is no longer mortified by comparisons between her
sisters' beauty and her own. But it is most pleasant to hear
in the last chapter that Miss Bingley was "very deeply mortified" by Darcy's marriage, for it is a treatment she long has
been needing; but that as she thought it advisable to retain
the right of visiting Pemberley she was wise enough to drop
all "resentment" and pay off arrears of civility to Elizabeth.
Even she has profited from the mortification, but, necessarily, only to the degree she is capable, a degree of meanness.

The Hero and the Villain

Andrew H. Wright

Andrew H. Wright claims that Darcy deserves the title of hero for his friendship with Bingley, his humility following Elizabeth's criticism, and his arrangements for Wickham's and Lydia's marriage. Wright describes Wickham, on the other hand, as a handsome, charming villain who proposes to women for their dowries. Both, however, are seen first through Elizabeth's faulty vision. Andrew H. Wright has taught English at Ohio State University and the University of California at San Diego. He is the author of a book on William Blake and *Henry Fielding: Mask and Feast*.

In *Pride and Prejudice*, hero and villain have prominent, interesting, and convincing parts. Each is present throughout the novel, both attract the heroine, and both receive the marital fates which they deserve. Elizabeth Bennet is a complicated and penetrating heroine; the two men with whom she associates herself romantically must also be intricate and intelligent.

If . . . Elizabeth's prejudices are views in which she takes pride, so ought it be said that Darcy's pride leads to prejudice. But even this is an over-simplification: his austerity of manner, as we learn from his housekeeper at Pemberley, stems partly from an inordinate shyness. It is impossible, however, to explain away his famous remark about Elizabeth (". . . tolerable; but not handsome enough to tempt *me* . . .'") on the grounds of diffidence alone—nor, indeed, the statement that '"My good opinion once lost is lost for ever"', nor the first proposal to Elizabeth; nor his subsequent explanatory letter. He *is* a proud man.

One way in which Jane Austen delineates his character is through his relationship with Bingley. It is partly through

From *Jane Austen's Novels*, by Andrew H. Wright (London: Chatto & Windus, 1953). Reprinted by permission of the publisher.

this friendship that a certain completeness is given to Darcy's character. Although we are struck, at the very beginning of the book, with Darcy's rudeness and with his pride, we may overlook the solidity of temperament implied in his affection for Bingley.

Despite his early bad impression of Elizabeth, he is soon constrained to like her better: for, ironically, the heroine by behaving disdainfully to him, does just what is necessary to captivate him. Thus at Sir William Lucas's party, her refusal to dance with him only sets him to thinking of her attractiveness; her piquancy at Netherfield leads to the famous conversation in which Elizabeth, while acknowledging that '"I dearly love a laugh"', insists that '"I hope I never ridicule what is wise or good"'—and from there to Darcy's increased awareness of 'the danger of paying Elizabeth too much attention'.

ELIZABETH'S REJECTION HUMBLES DARCY

The next appearance of Darcy comes when Elizabeth is visiting Hunsford, where she has gone to fulfil an unwilling promise of spending some time with Charlotte and William Collins. Besides the unfortunate first impression which the squire of Pemberley has made, there is now the insistent and plausible evidence against his character which Wickham has adduced. Elizabeth cannot understand the why of Darcy's repeated calls at the parsonage, nor can she comprehend the astonishing regularity of their 'unexpected' encounters in the Park. And she is stunned by his declaration of love, and proposal of marriage (critics who censure Jane Austen for an alleged lack of emotion should re-read this chapter).

> Elizabeth's astonishment was beyond expression. She stared, coloured, doubted, and was silent. This he considered sufficient encouragement, and the avowal of all that he felt and had long felt for her, immediately followed. He spoke well, but there were feelings besides those of the heart to be detailed, and he was not more eloquent on the subject of tenderness than of pride. His sense of her inferiority—of its being a degradation—of the family obstacles which judgment had always opposed to inclination, were dwelt on with a warmth which seemed due to the consequence he was wounding, but was very unlikely to recommend his suit.

> In spite of her deeply-rooted dislike, she could not be insensible to the compliment of such a man's affection, and though her intentions did not vary for an instant, she was at first sorry for the pain he was to receive; till, roused to resentment by his subsequent language, she lost all compas-

sion in anger. She tried, however, to compose herself to answer him with patience, when he should have done. He concluded with representing to her the strength of that attachment which, in spite of all his endeavours, he had found impossible to conquer; and with expressing his hope that it would now be rewarded by her acceptance of his hand. As he said this, she could easily see that he had no doubt of a favourable answer. He *spoke* of apprehension and anxiety, but his countenance expressed real security. Such a circumstance could only exasperate farther.

Elizabeth's angry refusal marks the beginning of the great change in Darcy: he is humbled, though there is but one sentence in the letter which he writes to her, to indicate that he has been mollified: 'I will only add, God bless you'.

Now he disappears from view, until Elizabeth, together with the Gardiners, visits Pemberley. Here Elizabeth's opinion of him softens slightly. And in fact there are a series of circumstances which disclose him to be a much more human person than she has previously thought him.

But this is not all: he behaves heroically, for he hastens to London, seeks out Lydia and Wickham, makes a provision for them, and all but drags them to the altar. These things he does not out of admiration for the eloped couple, but out of love for Elizabeth—which, however, he does not again bring himself to declare, until after Lady Catherine de Bourgh's interview with Elizabeth. This '"taught me to hope'", and so he is able to propose again, this time with success.

ELIZABETH WARNED OF WICKHAM

George Wickham is at once the most plausible and the most villainous of Jane Austen's anti-heroes: he is handsome, persuasive, personable; disingenuous, calculating, and dishonourable. His appearance in the story comes just as Elizabeth, smarting from Darcy's disapprobation, willingly abrogates her critical faculties in favour of a pleasant countenance and manner. She all too readily believes the militia lieutenant's defamation of Darcy's character—though we, the readers, are expected to take note of the warning signals which Elizabeth ignores. In the first place, Jane Bennet declares:

> It is impossible. No man of common humanity, no man who had any value for his character, could be capable of it. Can his most intimate friends be so excessively deceived in him? Oh! no.

In the second place, Miss Bingley plainly warns Elizabeth about Wickham, and indicates his relationship to Darcy:

So, Miss Eliza, I hear you are quite delighted with George Wickham!—Your sister has been talking to me about him, and asking me a thousand questions; and I find that the young man forgot to tell you, among his other communications, that he was the son of old Wickham, the late Mr. Darcy's steward. Let me recommend you, however, as a friend, not to give implicit confidence to all his assertions; for as to Mr. Darcy's using him ill, it is perfectly false; for, on the contrary, he has been always remarkably kind to him, though George Wickham has treated Mr. Darcy in a most infamous manner.

Jane Austen does not stack the cards, but she is not averse to throwing sand in her readers' eyes: both Jane and Miss Bingley are, as it happens, perfectly correct here; but Elizabeth does not believe either of them, for Jane's unwillingness ever to be unkind does sometimes blind her to people's faults, and Caroline Bingley's careless, insensitive stupidity often leads to complete misapprehension.

So Elizabeth continues to think well of Wickham, and ill of Darcy—even when the former announces his engagement to Miss King, whose dowry is £10,000. This time the heroine ignores the testimony—or rather, the conjecture— of one whose judgment she has always trusted: her aunt, Mrs. Gardiner.

'If [says Mrs. Gardiner] you will only tell me what sort of girl Miss King is, I shall know what to think.'

'She is a very good kind of girl, I believe. I know no harm of her.'

'But he paid her not the smallest attention, till her grandfather's death made her mistress of this fortune.'

'No—why should he? If it was not allowable for him to gain *my* affections, because I had no money, what occasion could there be for making love to a girl whom he did not care about, and who was equally poor?'

'But there seems indelicacy in directing his attentions towards her, so soon after this event.'

'A man in distressed circumstances has not time for all those elegant decorums which other people may observe. If *she* does not object to it, why should *we*?'

'*Her* not objecting, does not justify *him*. It only shews her being deficient in something herself—sense or feeling.'

'Well,' cried Elizabeth, 'have it as you choose. *He* shall be mercenary, and *she* shall be foolish.'

TRUTH ABOUT AND JUSTICE FOR WICKHAM

Although she is still unbelieving, however, Elizabeth will remember the doubts which she quashed in her early enthusiasm for Wickham—which, after all, arose partly out of her disdain for Darcy. Her big change dates from her second reading of Darcy's letter; then she excoriates herself for her blindness—though she cannot be expected to have guessed the full measure of Wickham's evil: his complete misrepresentation of Darcy, his planned elopement with Georgiana, his dissipated existence in London.

WICKHAM EXPLOITS DARCY'S SISTER

In his letter to Elizabeth, Darcy refutes Wickham's false accusations against him and explains how, after squandering the generous college allowance Darcy's father had given him, Wickham tried to elope with Darcy's fifteen-year-old sister for her fortune.

How he lived I know not. But last summer he was again most painfully obtruded on my notice. I must now mention a circumstance which I would wish to forget myself, and which no obligation less than the present should induce me to unfold to any human being. Having said thus much, I feel no doubt of your secrecy. My sister, who is more than ten years my junior, was left to the guardianship of my mother's nephew, Colonel Fitzwilliam, and myself. About a year ago, she was taken from school, and an establishment formed for her in London; and last summer she went with the lady who presided over it, to Ramsgate; and thither also went Mr. Wickham, undoubtedly by design; for there proved to have been a prior acquaintance between him and Mrs. Younge, in whose character we were most unhappily deceived; and by her connivance and aid, he so far recommended himself to Georgiana, whose affectionate heart retained a strong impression of his kindness to her as a child, that she was persuaded to believe herself in love, and to consent to an elopement. She was then but fifteen, which must be her excuse; and after stating her imprudence, I am happy to add, that I owed the knowledge of it to herself. I joined them unexpectedly a day or two before the intended elopement, and then Georgiana, unable to support the idea of grieving and offending a brother whom she almost looked up to as a father, acknowledged the whole to me. You may imagine what I felt and how I acted. Regard for my sister's credit and feelings prevented any public exposure, but I wrote to Mr. Wickham, who left the place immediately, and Mrs. Younge was of course removed from her charge. Mr. Wickham's chief object was unquestionably my sister's fortune, which is thirty thousand pounds; but I cannot help supposing that the hope of revenging himself on me, was a strong inducement. His revenge would have been complete indeed.

Jane Austen, *Pride and Prejudice*

He gets the fate which he deserves: he marries Lydia, after causing great distress to everyone concerned, except the foolish young girl herself. But, true to his character, he does not lose an ounce of aplomb. On this visit to Longbourn

> his manners were always so pleasing, that had his character and his marriage been exactly what they ought, his smiles and his easy address, while he claimed their relationship, would have delighted them all. Elizabeth had not before believed him quite equal to such assurance; but she sat down, resolving within herself, to draw no limits in future to the impudence of an impudent man.

Darcy and Wickham are virtually perfect agents of illusionment, and thus of the ironic theme, in *Pride and Prejudice*. Elizabeth is put off by Darcy's rudeness; her vanity is piqued: but she allows herself to over-emphasize his pride, because she comes so dangerously near to involvement with him. She credits Wickham's testimony because it is congenial to her—she misapprehends him because she wants to avoid entanglement with Darcy, while in fact there is nothing to fear from her relationship to Wickham: she is essentially indifferent to him. Thus her clarity of perception, which she genuinely possesses, contains the germs of its own myopia—ironically, when engagement of her affections is threatened.

Minor Female Characters Depict Women's Roles

Oliver MacDonagh

Oliver MacDonagh analyzes the minor female characters of small means in *Pride and Prejudice* to reveal how their circumstances affect marriages.
While Elizabeth and her sister Jane have the good
fortune to marry for romantic reasons, the minor
characters do not. They may opt to train for marriageable accomplishments, choose a loveless but fi-
nancially secure marriage, face spinsterhood, or risk
social disgrace. Oliver MacDonagh, a student of literature and of Irish history and culture, is the author
of *Ireland, Irish Culture, and Nationalism,
1750–1950,* and *States of Mind: A Study of Anglo-
Irish Conflict, 1780–1980.*

In *Pride and Prejudice* Charlotte stands in opposition to Elizabeth Bennet as the proponent, even if *faute de mieux*,[1] of 'career' marriage for women. Although 'sensible, intelligent'
and Elizabeth's chosen friend, she deliberately angles for a
match with the sycophantic bore Collins, 'solely from the
pure and disinterested desire of an establishment[;] . . . marriage had always been her object; it was the only honourable
provision for well-educated young women of small fortune,
and however uncertain of giving happiness, must be their
pleasantest preservative from want'. She is not so hardened
in prosaicness as to be quite free of shame in communicating the success of her endeavour to Elizabeth. On Elizabeth's
cry of anguished astonishment, she

> gave way to a momentary confusion here on receiving so di-
> rect a reproach; though, as it was no more than she expected,
> she soon regained her composure, and calmly replied, 'Why

1. for want of better

should you be surprised, my dear Eliza?—Do you think it in-
credible that Mr Collins should be able to procure any
woman's good opinion, because he was not so happy as to
succeed with you?'

CHARLOTTE'S DEFENCE OF HER MARRIAGE PLANS

Charlotte proceeds to cover over the awkwardness of the
revelation by attributing Elizabeth's exclamation to surprise
at Mr Collins proposing marriage to a second woman within
three days of being rejected by the first. She then expounds
the classic female defence of the loveless match:

> But when you have had time to think it all over, I hope you
> will be satisfied with what I have done. I am not romantic you
> know. I never was. I ask only a comfortable home; and con-
> sidering Mr Collins's character, connections, and situation in
> life, I am convinced that my chance of happiness with him is
> as fair, as most people can boast on entering the marriage
> state.

Elizabeth makes no further protest, but privately her censure of Charlotte knew no measure. She had 'sacrificed
every better feeling to worldly advantage'; she had 'dis-
graced' herself; 'Charlotte the wife of Mr Collins, was a most
humiliating picture!'. Moreover, it was impossible for Charlotte to be even 'tolerably happy in the lot she had chosen'.

Jane Austen does not however allow this somewhat dramatic view of 'career' marriage a complete walk-over. It is evident from the later description of life in her new home at
Hunsford that Charlotte is pleased with her bargain. Granted,
this owes a great deal to her skill in diverting her husband
from her side. She encourages him, literally, to cultivate his
garden, which draws him outside for many hours. She also
sees to it that he has the better parlour for his study because
this faces the road and affords him the amusement of watching such spectacles as the highway offers. Elizabeth 'soon saw
that her friend had an excellent reason for what she did, for
Mr Collins would undoubtedly have been much less in his
own apartment, had they sat in one equally lively; and she
gave Charlotte credit for the arrangement'. Similarly, Collins's
blunders and pomposity should have repeatedly put his wife
to the blush, 'but in general Charlotte wisely did not hear'.
Thus between closing her parlour door and her ears sufficiently often on her husband, Mrs Collins manages to extract
a great deal of happiness from her new condition. Her delight
is her pleasant home and domestic responsibilities. . . .

MARRIAGE AS A PRAGMATIC ISSUE

The merging of individuals in a new joint interest both emphasized and symbolized the social character of marriage. Charlotte's ultimate justification lay in her obedience to the social law which laid down that middle-class young women without resources tended to be lonely, purposeless and very poor if they could not attain such a union. Even the soft-judging Jane Bennet recognizes the force of this particular law when she expostulates at Elizabeth's unbridled condemnation of Charlotte's engagement, and warns of the ill-consequences of wholesale indulgence in high principle.

> My dear Lizzy, do not give way to such feelings as these. They will ruin your happiness. You do not make allowance enough for difference of situation and temper. Consider Mr Collins's respectability, and Charlotte's prudent, steady character. Remember that she is one of a large family; that as to fortune, it is a most eligible match; and be ready to believe, for every body's sake, that she may feel something like regard and esteem for our cousin.

. . . No less than Elizabeth, Jane Bennet makes a romantic marriage, and we may perhaps infer that even Kitty Bennet, under the influence of her elder sisters, will eventually adopt their principles. Correspondingly, it is the novel's villain, George Wickham, who becomes the exemplar of the market view of marriage. He has tried to sell his charm to Georgiana Darcy for her £30,000, and turns his attentions from Elizabeth to Mary King when he comes to believe that Mary has a fortune. Finally, he allows himself to be bribed—rather cheaply—into making an honest woman of Lydia Bennet. Yet although romantic marriage is clearly the ideal in *Pride and Prejudice*, pragmatic marriage is presented as common practice, if not in fact the commonest. In defending it, Charlotte Lucas had a particularly poor case to argue. She could make no pretence of prior affection for Mr Collins, and tacitly admitted that any woman of sense would find his company 'irksome'. But was the alternative—penurious, occupationless and perhaps unloved spinsterhood, at best fitting into the interstices of relations' lives—a better fate? . . .

THE PROBLEM OF GETTING SINGLE WOMEN SETTLED

In every sense, girls are the problem in *Pride and Prejudice*. The Bennets' superfluity of daughters and lack of a male heir form the book's central difficulty. The Lucases share the

CHARLOTTE'S PRAGMATIC MARRIAGE

Charlotte's engagement to Mr. Collins pleases her entire family for its financial benefits, with no considerations of Charlotte's happiness.

Miss Lucas, who accepted him solely from the pure and disinterested desire of an establishment, cared not how soon that establishment were gained.

Sir William and Lady Lucas were speedily applied to for their consent; and it was bestowed with a most joyful alacrity. Mr. Collins's present circumstances made it a most eligible match for their daughter, to whom they could give little fortune; and his prospects of future wealth were exceedingly fair. . . . The whole family in short were properly overjoyed on the occasion. The younger girls formed hopes of *coming out* a year or two sooner than they might otherwise have done; and the boys were relieved from their apprehension of Charlotte's dying an old maid. Charlotte herself was tolerably composed. She had gained her point, and had time to consider of it. Her reflections were in general satisfactory. Mr. Collins to be sure was neither sensible nor agreeable; his society was irksome, and his attachment to her must be imaginary. But still he would be her husband.

Jane Austen, *Pride and Prejudice*

first part of this difficulty, in a lesser form. Miss Darcy has been (and to some extent still is) a problem for her brother. Miss Bingley's problem is to dispose of herself as she desires. The heiresses, great and small, Anne de Bourgh and Mary King, are problems for their mothers to dispose of. At least eight girls in the novel (stretching the term 'girl' to cover at least a twelve-year span in age) are fully, or fairly fully, delineated. Their characters and prospects vary widely. But all pose essentially the same question to themselves or others— how were they to be settled in the world?

The Bennet girls form the book's core group. Each has the identical disadvantage of a negligible dowry (£1,000 at most after their parents' deaths) and the prospect of a calamitous decline in social significance after their middle-aged father dies and the family estate passes into other hands. . . . The first pair are much the more finely and intricately drawn as characters, but the respective roles are substantially the same. Elizabeth is three years older than Catherine, far more sophisticated, far cleverer, wittier and . . . probably much the better read. Yet she undergoes a similar change to

Catherine. Albeit at greater depth at each particular stage, she grows from girlhood to young womanhood during the novel's span. . . .

INCORRIGIBLE LYDIA

Lydia's was a deteriorating course. She is introduced as a handsome, 'stout, well-grow girl of fifteen, with . . . high animal spirits, and a sort of natural self-consequence', but also silly, reckless and wild. These traits have been thoroughly displayed, in speech and conduct, by the time that Elizabeth, after absorbing Darcy's condemnation of the majority of the family, elaborates it (and Kitty's subordinate character) in a dispirited reverie.

> Her father, contented with laughing at them, would never exert himself to restrain the wild giddiness of his youngest daughters; and her mother, with manners so far from right herself, was entirely insensible of the evil . . . while they were supported by their mother's indulgence, what chance could there be of improvement? Catherine, weak-spirited, irritable, and completely under Lydia's guidance, had been always affronted by their advice; and Lydia, self-willed and careless, would scarcely give them a hearing. They were ignorant, idle, and vain.

None the less, Elizabeth makes a last vicarious attempt at Lydia's reform. At home, she appeals to her father to intervene while there yet was time.

> If you, my dear father, will not take the trouble of checking her exuberant spirits, and of teaching her that her present pursuits are not to be the business of her life, she will soon be beyond the reach of amendment. Her character will be fixed, and she will, at sixteen, be the most determined flirt that ever made herself and her family ridiculous . . . from the ignorance and emptiness of her mind, wholly unable to ward off any portion of that universal contempt which her rage for admiration will excite. In this danger Kitty is also comprehended. She will follow wherever Lydia leads. Vain, ignorant, idle, and absolutely uncontrouled!

But, as ever, Mr Bennet laughed his way out of his family obligations, and Lydia more than realized Elizabeth's fears by eloping and then living 'in sin' with Wickham. Lydia was irredeemable. She returned to Longbourn, quite without consciousness of her wrongdoing, in fact glorying in her near-shotgun wedding. 'Lydia was Lydia still; untamed, unabashed, wild, noisy, and fearless'. Her character was fixed: she retained, in later years, 'all the claims to reputation which her marriage had given her'. . . .

What of models as a contributory explanation of the divergence between the sisters? Despite her vigour and independent spirit, Elizabeth seriously respected, and even acknowledged the moral superiority of her elder sister Jane, who was close to her in age and interest. Are we meant to infer that Jane exerted a moderating influence on Elizabeth, perhaps even acted as her second conscience? Bitterly did she reproach herself, after Darcy had opened her eyes to the truth about Wickham and his family, that she had so '"often disdained the generous candour of my sister, and gratified my vanity, in useless or blameable distrust"'. . . . Lydia however was not a girl for models, and Mrs Bennet's example could have done little more than license and accentuate her headlong self-indulgence. Contrariwise, Lydia dominated Kitty, the sister next to her in age, affording a deplorable but powerful model of one particular form of ill-reared girl.

The principal differentiating factor for Jane Austen was, however, education—including of course self-education. She makes it clear that this was sufficiently available to the Bonnet girls, in what the Victorians would have termed a 'permissive but not compulsory' form. '"Do you play and sing?"', Lady Catherine demanded of Elizabeth. . . .

Lydia, however, was chief among those who had chosen to be idle. Both Elizabeth and Mr Bennet call her 'ignorant' repeatedly; and her speech is occasionally ungrammatical as well as vulgar. Three times in succession she says 'Kitty and me' for 'Kitty and I' in describing their adventures when meeting Jane from the London coach. . . . Evidently, then, the familiar climbing frame for girls' education was available to the Bennets—the fresh moral being that those who would not make the effort to train themselves must be both disciplined and set good example if they were not to end as frivolous and ill-formed as Lydia.

UPBRINGING BY ACCOMPLISHMENTS

The 'accomplishments' type of girls' upbringing is dealt with as scathingly as the dark side of the *laissez-faire*[2] 'system'. Its prime exemplars in *Pride and Prejudice* are Mrs Hurst and Miss Bingley. They 'had been educated in one of the first private seminaries in town', whence they emerged not only 'very fine ladies; not deficient in . . . the power of being

2. noninterference; left alone

agreeable where they chose it' but also 'proud and con-
ceited', and devotees of frippery, and tawdry cultural adorn-
ment, as the hallmarks of the lady. Mary Bennet is another
professor of the creed of feminine accomplishments, an
autodidact in the field. But in her case talentless 'playing and
singing' and banal 'philosophy' represent only the desperate
attempt of a plain girl to make some standing room for herself in the midst of a family of pretty sisters. Once the com-
petitive pressure is relaxed, so too is Mary's devotion to her
superficial acquirements. When she was at last the only girl
regularly at home, she was 'necessarily drawn from the pursuit of accomplishments by Mrs Bennet's being quite unable
to sit alone . . . and as she was no longer mortified by comparisons between her sisters' beauty and her own, it was
suspected by her father that she submitted to the change
without much reluctance'.

Mary was not the only girl in the novel to be improved by
a change in her circumstances in her later years, although in
the cases of Georgiana Darcy and Kitty Bennet the change
was essentially an improvement in their social training. After
her brother's marriage, Georgiana left her chaperon-
governess in London to live at Pemberley. She 'had the highest opinion in the world of Elizabeth' from whom she learned
a new sort of tact and discrimination. Kitty also spent much
of her time with Elizabeth and most of the remainder with
Jane, now Mrs Bingley. Living with such sisters worked 'to
her very material advantage. . . . In society so superior to
what she had generally known, her improvement was
great . . . removed from the influence of Lydia's example, she
became, by proper attention and management, less irritable,
less ignorant, and less insipid'. Even at seventeen or eighteen
years of age, a girl such as Kitty might still be saved.

Dissimilar in every other way, Charlotte Lucas resembles
Lydia in pursuing her chosen course unwaveringly to the
end. As we have seen, her first private words to Elizabeth
laid out her credo, that, with or without affection, it was the
business of girls to scheme themselves into marriage, the
outcome being, in terms of happiness, altogether a question
of luck. As we have also seen, Jane Austen allows Charlotte
to elaborate fairly her own defence. Better still, she later
finds her a most generous advocate in Jane Bennet, when
Elizabeth denounces Charlotte's marriage as '"in every
view . . . unaccountable"'.

ELIZABETH HAS THE LAST WORD

But Jane Austen could not wholly suppress her partiality for Elizabeth and her standpoint. 'I must confess', she wrote, not altogether in play, when *Pride and Prejudice* was published, 'that I think her as delightful a creature as ever appeared in print, and how I shall be able to tolerate those who do not like *her* at least I do not know'. Elizabeth must be given the last word. '"You shall not defend her, though it is Charlotte Lucas"', she answered her elder sister. '"You shall not, for the sake of one individual, change the meaning of principle and integrity, nor endeavour to persuade yourself or me, that selfishness is prudence, and insensibility of danger, security for happiness"'. Charlotte must be condemned for her betrayal of the very first principle of girlhood, the integrity of the heart. Was a female education which ended in cold rationality any better after all than those ending in heedless self-gratification or tinkling vanities? It is surely not by chance that Jane Austen anticipates the day when Charlotte's household delights at Hunsford will lose their charm or that she leaves Charlotte pregnant—by Mr Collins—in the end.

CHAPTER 3

Structure and Plot

The Relationship Between Author and Reader

John Odmark

John Odmark shows how Austen controls the reader's knowledge or lack of it. What does this mean? Austen creates dialogue that gives the reader knowledge superior to that of the characters, dialogue ambiguous enough to leave room for further character development, and dialogue that foreshadows events. For his doctoral dissertation, submitted to the University of Regensberg in Germany, John Odmark researched the ways Austen's novels bridge the distance between author and reader. He edited a collection of criticism, *Language, Literature, and Meaning*, before his death.

Jane Austen has been accused of a fundamental incoherence of point of view; however, if her commitment to maintaining a consistently ironic perspective is kept in mind, apparent inconsistencies in the point of view are for the most part eliminated. . . . Jane Austen has the advantage over the reader in that she knows at any given point in the narrative the extent of the reader's familiarity with the characters and events being portrayed, and, as a consequence, she can anticipate what the reader's expectations and possible responses are likely to be. . . .

CONTROLLING DISTANCE BETWEEN THE READER AND EVENTS

The narrator's position is clearly defined and unchanging. He has limited omniscience, that is, he does not tell all he presumably knows. The necessity of controlling the distance between the reader and the events being portrayed determines what is revealed and what is withheld. This of course includes what is implied but left unsaid. Each of the heroines undergoes an educational process which leads her to perceive her own error in the light of an objective reality. . . .

Enough distance is established to prevent the reader from viewing the heroine uncritically, but not so much as to lose the reader's sympathy for her. In other words, the primary source of Jane Austen's irony derives from knowledge or a lack of it. This is true not only in regard to the heroines but in regard to the other characters as well. The author builds up the ironies in her novels on the discrepancies between the reader's knowledge and that of the characters on the one hand and the reader's knowledge and that of the narrator on the other. . . .

[Austen's] commentary, which is less obtrusive than [novelist Henry] Fielding's, provides an ironic perspective on the heroines' evaluation of their own behaviour and that of others. Some of the commentary is stated directly by the narrator, but it is often merely implied through juxtaposition, selection, or the indirect presentation of conversation. . . .

In any given dramatic exchange, one of Jane Austen's characters is likely to have 'superior' knowledge, which is not the same as to suggest that he is morally or socially superior. Quite the contrary may in fact be the case. Rarely in Jane Austen are both parties equally informed and equally in control of the situation. . . . The author prefers situations in which one of the parties dominates. This dominance may have positive or negative consequences, but in either case it is most probable that effective communication takes place only in one direction. The dominant speaker may be aware of some weakness in his listener's character, such as pride or foolishness, or may know that he himself is lying or at least withholding information—to cite only a few of the possibilities. One speaker's knowledge is superior to the other's, but the reader's knowledge is superior to them both. This superiority is partly due to the reader's experience of the text up to this point, and to the explicit or at least implicit commentary in the scene itself. . . .

WHO KNOWS WHAT IN THE OPENING SCENE

The first chapter of *Pride and Prejudice* might be summarized as follows:

> Mrs Bennet announces that an eligible young bachelor has moved into the neighbourhood, and she suggests to her husband that he should pay a call on their new neighbour, since

it almost certainly will be decisive for the future of one of their five daughters. Mr Bennet rejects the proposal.

What is missing from this summary is the irony which operates at three levels: Mrs Bennet's interpretation of other people's remarks and the new situation created by the presence of an eligible young man; Mr Bennet's responses to his wife; and the ironic perspective established by the narrator, which provides the reader with a knowledge superior to Mr Bennet's, whose knowledge is, in turn, superior to his wife's. The opening sentence is an assertion: 'It is a truth universally acknowledged, that a single man in possession of a good fortune must be in want of a wife.' The word order undercuts the validity of the assertion being made, since an illogical conclusion follows upon what appears to be a statement of fact. This statement is not put into Mrs Bennet's mouth, and it is only in the course of the ensuing scene that it becomes clearly identified with her perception of the situation and, more generally, the quality of her mind. As becomes apparent immediately, logic is not one of her strong points. The principals do such a good job of giving themselves away at every turn in this scene that there is little need for the narrator to intervene.

> However little known the feelings or views of such a man may be on his first entering a neighbourhood, this truth is so well fixed in the minds of the surrounding families, that he is considered as the rightful property of some one or other of their daughters.
>
> Mr Bennet replied that he had not.
>
> Mr Bennet made no answer.
>
> This was invitation enough.
>
> Mr Bennet was so odd a mixture of quick parts, sarcastic humour, reserve, and caprice, that the experience of three and twenty years had been insufficient to make his wife understand his character. Her mind was less difficult to develope. She was a woman of mean understanding, little information, and uncertain temper. When she was discontented she fancied herself nervous. The business of her life was to get her daughters married; its solace was visiting and news.

The narrator's comments provide a structural frame for the scene between Mr and Mrs Bennet. These subdued remarks are in striking contrast to Mrs Bennet's. Further, they reflect the narrator's partisanship in favour of the husband. The last of the narrator's comments quoted above confirms what is already implicit in Mr Bennet's responses to his wife, that she is to be humoured but not taken seriously. Mrs Bennet's comments are comprised of nonsense, which may be sub-divided into questions, assertions, and hearsay. While her husband has no difficulty in comprehending her point long before she has made it, Mrs Bennet remains ignorant to the end of the true import of her spouse's remarks. Her asser-tions and relations of hearsay are not taken at face value. She is incapable of anticipating her husband's responses. As communicative acts Mrs Bennet's remarks are not success-ful, since the receiver, Mr Bennet, refuses to interpret the message as the sender has intended. In the other direction, communication does not function much better. Mr Bennet is obviously aware that his remarks will be misunderstood. The irony of course is that it is Mr Bennet's intention that his remarks be misconstrued. The narrator's comments which underline the ironic implications of this scene provide a per-spective of superior knowledge, which the reader shares with the narrator throughout the rest of the novel.

THE READER'S ASSESSMENT AND REASSESSMENT OF THE FIRST ELIZABETH-DARCY SCENES

From this perspective the reader has to assess and reassess what he learns. The distance established between him and the heroine places the reader in a more favourable position than Elizabeth Bennet to recognize where there has been misunderstanding, though the ironic implications of such misunderstandings only become evident in retrospect. The action turns on the misunderstandings which exist not only for the reader but also for the participants in the action. The development of the plot depends on the effectiveness of the scenes between Elizabeth and Darcy. These are the reader's best opportunity to assess Darcy's thoughts and feelings. Some critics have argued that Darcy's transformation is un-convincing, that he is manipulated by the author for the sake of the plot and does not come across as a fully-rounded, be-lievable character. This line of argument overlooks two im-portant points. In the first place, the reader views Darcy from Elizabeth's not unprejudiced perspective. Secondly, the changes in his attitude are carefully prepared for. The key scenes involving Darcy and Elizabeth are subject to more than one interpretation. Elizabeth gives them the reading which corresponds to the prejudices she forms at their first meeting.

ASSESSING ELIZABETH'S FIRST IMPRESSIONS OF DARCY

At the first Netherfield ball, Elizabeth overhears Darcy's unflattering comments referring to her. To Bingley's suggestion that Darcy be introduced to Elizabeth, Darcy responds, 'She is tolerable, but not handsome enough to tempt me; and I am in no humour at present to give consequence to young ladies who are slighted by other men. You had better return to your partner and enjoy her smiles, for you are wasting your time with me'. . . .

Somewhat later in the course of the action, when Sir William Lucas attempts to bring Darcy and Elizabeth together, it becomes clear that Elizabeth's view of Darcy for the time being has been fixed by her 'first impression'; whereas there are hints already at this early stage that his view of Elizabeth has begun to alter under the influence of closer observation.

> 'My dear Eliza, why are you not dancing? Mr Darcy, you must allow me to present this young lady to you as a very desirable partner.—You cannot refuse to dance, I am sure, when so much beauty is before you.' And taking her hand, he would have given it to Mr Darcy, who, though extremely surprised, was not unwilling to receive it, when she instantly drew back, and said with some discomposure to Sir William,
>
> 'Indeed, Sir, I have not the least intention of dancing.—I entreat you not to suppose that I moved this way in order to beg for a partner.'
>
> Mr Darcy with grave propriety requested to be allowed the honour of her hand; but in vain. Elizabeth was determined; nor did Sir William at all shake her purpose by his attempt at persuasion.
>
> 'You excel so much in the dance, Miss Eliza, that it is cruel to deny me the happiness of seeing you; and though this gentleman dislikes the amusement in general, he can have no objection, I are sure, to oblige us for one half hour.'
>
> 'Mr Darcy is all politeness,' said Elizabeth, smiling.
>
> 'He is indeed—but considering the inducement, my dear Eliza, we cannot wonder at his complaisance; for who would object to such a partner?'
>
> Elizabeth looked archly, and turned away. Her resistance had not injured her with the gentleman.

The most significant feature of this scene is how little either Elizabeth or Darcy says. Sir William is well-meaning, but his remarks are only a too vivid reminder to Elizabeth of Darcy's previous lack of interest in dancing with her. Her statement 'Mr Darcy is all politeness' is not clearly marked; that is, it signals a number of possible interpretations, ranging from insult to compliment. It is intentionally ironic, but it may be even more ironic than the speaker assumes. The proffered partner may indeed wish to dance with Elizabeth and not only because of the exigencies of the situation created by Sir William and the rules of decorum but for more personal reasons. The reader, however, cannot be certain. Darcy's request for a dance is not given but only referred to. From it the reader might have been able to deduce more concerning Darcy's motives. His thoughts at the end of the scene are recorded by the narrator, but these are a response to Elizabeth's reaction to the situation. What he was thinking prior to her 'resistance' is only hinted at with the phrase, 'not unwilling to receive it', meaning Elizabeth's hand for the dance. The technique of presentation in this scene is more complex than anything in the earlier novels or even in the first chapter of *Pride and Prejudice*, where the speeches of Mr and Mrs Bennet are still clearly marked. None of the participants controls the conversation or fully comprehends its implications, not even the reader. Sir William is completely oblivious to any deeper significance whatever. Darcy may perceive some of Elizabeth's irony, but not all of it, for he is unaware of the fact that she has already formed a very definite opinion of him. Elizabeth fails to recognize that Darcy's invitation might be anything more than a courteous gesture.

AMBIGUOUS SCENES ANTICIPATE FUTURE ACTION

As the story progresses, Jane Austen continues to utilize the ambiguities of such situations for purposes of characterization and in anticipation of the climactic point where Elizabeth perceives her own error.

> Mr Darcy drawing near Elizabeth said to her—
> 'Do not you feel a great inclination, Miss Bennet, to seize such an opportunity of dancing a reel?'
> She smiled, but made no answer. He repeated the question, with some surprise at her silence.
> 'Oh!' said she, 'I heard you before; but I could not immediately determine what to say in reply. You wanted me, I know to say 'Yes,' that you might have the pleasure of despising my taste; but I always delight in overthrowing those kinds of schemes, and cheating a person of their premeditated contempt. I have therefore made up my mind to tell you, that I do not want to dance a reel at all—and now despise me if you dare.'
> 'Indeed I do not dare.'
> Elizabeth having rather expected to affront him, was amazed at his gallantry; but there was a mixture of sweetness

and archness in her manner which made it difficult for her to affront anybody; and Darcy had never been so bewitched by any woman as he was by her. He really believed, that were it not for the inferiority of her connections, he should be in some danger.

This scene is a variation on the last one quoted above. This time Darcy himself takes the initiative in asking Elizabeth to dance. Elizabeth attributes a motive to his request which is not impossible but is unlikely in the light of Darcy's further remark, which takes her by surprise. The narrator's comment increases rather than reduces the ambiguities of this scene. On the one hand it brings out clearly Darcy's sense of pride; on the other, it indicates that Elizabeth has become more than a subject of minor interest to him. The key question implied in this scene is why Darcy does not 'dare'. For the time being, it is left unanswered.

They stood for some time without speaking a word; and she began to imagine that their silence was to last through the two dances, and at first was resolved not to break it; till suddenly fancying that it would be greater punishment to her partner to oblige him to talk, she made some slight observation on the dance. He replied, and was again silent. After a pause of some minutes she addressed him a second time with

'It is *your* turn to say something now, Mr Darcy—I talked about the dance, and you ought to make some kind of remark on the size of the room, or the number of couples.'

He smiled, and assured her that whatever she wished him to say should be said.

'Very well.—That reply will do for the present.—Perhaps by and bye I may observe that private balls are much pleasanter than public ones.—But *now* we may remain silent.'

'Do you talk by the rule then, while you are dancing?'

'Sometimes. One must speak a little, you know. It would look odd to be entirely silent for half an hour together, and yet for the advantage of *some*, conversation ought to be so arranged as that they may have the trouble of saying as little as possible.'

'Are you consulting your own feelings in the present case, or do you imagine that you are gratifying mine?'

'Both,' replied Elizabeth archly; 'for I have always seen a great similarity in the turn of our minds.—We are each of an unsocial, taciturn disposition, unwilling to speak, unless we expect to say something that will amaze the whole room, and be handed down to posterity with all the eclat of a proverb.'

'This is not a very striking resemblance of your own character, I am sure,' said he. 'How near it may be to *mine*, I cannot pretend to say.—*You* think it a faithful portrait undoubtedly.'

'I must not decide on my own performance.'
He made no answer. . . .

Elizabeth's recent conversation with Wickham (Chapter 16) has confirmed her in her opinion of Darcy's pride. In this scene she sets out to bait him. Darcy is here even less able to discern Elizabeth's motives than he was in the previous scene. The stage is being prepared for the gross misunderstandings which lead to Darcy's first proposal and Elizabeth's refusal (Chapter 34). Soon after this encounter Darcy departs, not to meet Elizabeth again before she goes to visit her friend Charlotte and he to visit his aunt. He goes away more impressed than ever by Elizabeth's charm and wit, unaware that her opinion of him is far from favourable. For her part, in the interim, Elizabeth grasps at every bit of evidence against Darcy which is consistent with the image she has already formed of him. . . .

SCENES ALLOW MULTIPLE INTERPRETATIONS

In the scene above, Darcy's initial silence and subsequent civil responses are motivated by politeness, but also by a stronger feeling of which Elizabeth is unaware and the reader unsure. For example, the reader cannot be certain how to interpret Darcy's willingness to say whatever Elizabeth would like him to. Perhaps, Darcy is just matching Elizabeth in her facetiousness, but it is also possible that his 'willingness' is an indication of his growing interest in Elizabeth. Most of the remarks in this scene are marked in such a complex manner that intentions and responses are left unclear. Consequently, it is difficult to determine with certainty what each of the parties means to say, or what significance they assign to what they hear. . . .

Conversation as a social activity takes place, and none of the rules for correct behaviour are broken; but as subsequent events confirm, no real understanding between those involved occurs. The smiles, the silences, and the surprised reactions which are features of these encounters contribute to the ambiguities. Such ambiguities are not absent from the novels which were to follow; however, in none of the other novels is the development of the action so dependent upon them. For the first time, Jane Austen succeeds in integrating the local and the structural ironies. In *Northanger Abbey* local ironies are developed at the expense of the larger ironic pattern in the plot's structure. In *Sense and Sensibility* the structural ironies seem forced. In *Pride and Prejudice* Jane Austen continues to use to some extent techniques of presentation which she has employed earlier. She seldom uses an inside view, but whenever she does, it has the same function as in the other novels. In her handling of the dialogue of the secondary characters, for instance in the first chapter, the author's method is similar—if more complex and more frequently employed—to what she had done previously. But in her treatment of the two characters who are the focus of attention throughout most of the novel, and in the overall conception of the narrative, she also explores new possibilities of presentation.

The Narrator's Voice

Julia Prewitt Brown

Julia Prewitt Brown explains how the juxtaposition of action and dialogue with narrative voice reveals the author's voice. Brown notes that *Pride and Prejudice* opens with a direct address to the reader, a sentence that can be interpreted as comic or ironic. She argues that Austen's action and dialogue suggest disorder while the narrative voice is seemingly objective; the contrast between the two creates the same ambiguity and irony present in the opening sentence. Brown concludes that Austen's statement of moral and emotional intelligence is apparent at the end in the maturity of Elizabeth and Darcy. Julia Prewitt Brown, a Mellon fellow at Harvard University in 1979–1980, taught English at Boston University.

Certain moments in literature always surprise us, no matter how many times we encounter them. One such moment is Cordelia's response to Lear, "Nothing," in the first act of the tragedy. Another is the opening sentence of *Pride and Prejudice*: "It is a truth universally acknowledged, that a single man in possession of a good fortune must be in want of a wife". Like Cordelia's unexpected reply, Austen's claim is surprising because we do not know how to interpret it. . . .

The opening claim of *Pride and Prejudice* is either an instance of unalloyed irony or comic hyperbole. Read ironically, it means a great deal more than it says; read comically, it means a great deal less. Because its targets are unknown, its assurance is baffling. No matter how we read it, its finality is its irony (or comedy); it holds its "truth" and the resistance to its truth in one—the quintessential stance of the ironic comedies.

AMBIGUITY IN THE OPENING NARRATIVE AND DIALOGUE

Such instances are very few and brief in Jane Austen. They constitute a direct address from the author to the reader.

Reprinted by permission of the publisher from *Jane Austen's Novels: Social Change and Literary Form*, by Julia Prewitt Brown (Cambridge, MA: Harvard University Press). Copyright © 1979 by the President and Fellows of Harvard College.

They dazzle us partly because they are infrequent, and they provide in their flashing ambiguity a highly concentrated version of the novelist's perspective. The discourse of the rest of *Pride and Prejudice* issues from this initial stance and falls into two broad categories, narrative and dialogue. Perceived together, as they are meant to be perceived, the narrative and the dialogue achieve the same brilliant ambiguity of the authorial voice. Consider the first appearance of narrative comment in the novel, at the close of chapter 1:

> Mr. Bennet was so odd a mixture of quick parts, sarcastic humour, reserve, and caprice, that the experience of three and twenty years had been insufficient to make his wife understand his character. *Her* mind was less difficult to develop. She was a woman of mean understanding, little information, and uncertain temper. When she was discontented she fancied herself nervous. The business of her life was to get her daughters married; its solace was visiting and news.

Considered in isolation, the passage seems objective, informative, and unambiguous. Yet when read as the conclusion of the following dialogue, the passage achieves a different resonance:

> "My dear Mr. Bennet," said his lady to him one day, "have you heard that Netherfield is let at last?" Mr. Bennet replied that he had not.
> "But it is," returned she; "for Mrs. Long has just been here, and she told me all about it."
> Mr. Bennet made no answer.
> "Do not you want to know who has taken it?" cried his wife impatiently.
> "*You* want to tell me, and I have no objection to hearing it."
> This was invitation enough.

Here we have a world of opinion and report, and one in which the effect of an event takes the place of the event itself. Neither time nor place is specified except as "day" and "neighborhood." We have only the disembodied voices of wife and husband clashing in an empty space, and ricocheting back in the form of countless amplifying ironies to the novel's opening statement. The sensibility of the dialogue is ephemeral, irrational, opinionated; it is a precarious world indeed to be followed by such stable, definitive evaluations as "She was a woman of mean understanding" or such simplistic understatements as "Her mind was less difficult to develope." This ostensibly objective narrative voice is true as far as it goes. It is true because its evaluations are, as evaluations, correct and useful. They are the necessary simplifications we live by, and the Bennets live by, for the paragraph reveals each as seen by the other.

Yet these evaluations cannot be mistaken for life itself, and Jane Austen knows they cannot. When Elizabeth returns from visiting Mr. and Mrs. Collins and her mother asks whether they "do not often talk of having Longbourn when your father is dead," we are surprised. We are required once again to acknowledge the audacity and variety and complexity of this woman's "mean understanding." The cadence of moral rationalism, the abstract, judgmental sensibility revealed in such statements as "mean understanding, little information, and uncertain temper" are always checked by action and dialogue. Through the careful juxtaposition of narrative and dialogue, Austen prevents us from investing everything in such statements.

THE DANGERS OF SIMPLIFICATION

Elizabeth too must learn that simplifications are dangerous; both she and Darcy insist on what is only provisional and half-true as final. Of her complacent division of humanity into intricate and simple characters, for example, Elizabeth comes to say, "The more I see of the world, the more am I dissatisfied with it; and every day confirms me of the inconsistency of all human characters, and of the little dependence that can be placed on the appearance of either merit or sense". The irony of the novel's opening sentence lies in its assurance in simplification and generalization, its insistence that the local perception is universal, absolute, permanent. We simplify our world in order to live in it; and Austen . . . keeps telling us we do. *Pride and Prejudice* is an exhilarating work because it turns us back continually on life by showing us the failure of language and the individual mind to capture life's unexpectedness. And beneath the exhilaration lies an affection for the bizarre actuality of things. The opening hyperbole, for example, contains an element of eccentric delight in human exaggeration.

THE NARRATIVE VOICE DEFINES STRUCTURE; THE DIALOGUE AND ACTION DEFINE ANARCHY

The narrative voice, then, provides some limit, some barrier, which the action strives ceaselessly (and successfully) to overcome. The narrator's provision of certitude, despite its accuracy, is temporary. Nevertheless, its role in the novel is of vital importance. Indeed, without the narrative voice, the moral structure of the novel would crumble. The terms of order in the novel are defined by the narrative voice, just as the terms of anarchy are defined by dialogue and action. In this respect, Austen works in a way similar to that of George Eliot.[1] Eliot's compassionate narrative voice is used both to reprimand and to redeem the failing world of Middlemarch. Austen's rational narrative voice is used both to abuse and applaud the evasions of humankind—abuse the cruelties and applaud the abundance. Only through the careful and complex juxtaposition of action and narrative does each author maintain her ambiguity. The depth of both *Pride and Prejudice* and *Middlemarch* depends on the reader's sensitivity to the relationship between the action of the characters and the voice that enfolds it. . . .

In Austen, the "story" is made meaningful by narrative intrusion; and "description" or reflection is made meaningful by story. Jane Austen's narrative voice establishes a stability in a world of fluctuating opinions and exaggerations. . . .

The narrative voice, then, possesses the essential perspective of the novel. . . . It accepts in its embrace the evasions and irrationalities of direct dialogue and the cool, clear cadence of reason of the objective narrative. It brings them together in its brief flashes of genius, such as in the opening sentence of *Pride and Prejudice.* In such moments, the two streams of discourse in Jane Austen, narration and dialogue, rush together completely. They *represent* the effect of the novel, the total perspective we are to gain, one that rises spontaneously out of the interaction between narration and dialogue. . . .

Pride and Prejudice, however, deals less with the problem of accepting an inelegant and unpoetic world than with accepting an irrational and absurd one. If Emma's aspirations [in *Emma*]are for more witty and more alive surroundings, Elizabeth's efforts are to restrain the anarchic energies of cynicism and insensibility in her parents. The unrelenting invasion of sense by nonsense, of sensibility by moral nullity, of humor by nihilism is a dominant theme in the novel. . . .

THE WIDE GAP BETWEEN MRS. BENNET'S INTELLECTUAL ANARCHY AND ELIZABETH'S MORAL ORDER

The psychic and moral distances in the novel are enormous, while the physical distances are a matter of a coach ride. The internal distance between Elizabeth and her mother, for

---

1. pseudonym of Mary Ann Evans, author of the novels *Middlemarch, Silas Marner,* and others

example, we intuitively recognize to be a central structural element in the novel. Distances such as these establish the terms of sensibility and anarchy in the action. Yet what are the terms? Mrs. Bennet moves in an atmosphere of repugnance that is scarcely explained. Studies of Austen's language have insisted that the moral scale of the novels is located in speech—yet is this enough? The variations in diction and sentence structure provide clues to the moral scheme, but they should of course be connected to incident.

Mrs. Bennet and two other reprehensible characters, Lydia and Mr. Collins, as independent personalities, are each characterized by a failure to distinguish the important from the trivial, the valid from the invalid. In language and action, they have no true discriminating sense. Their failure is both intellectual and moral; part of the underlying philosophy of *Pride and Prejudice* is a belief in the intimate bond between intelligence and morality, articulated so well in [critic] Richard Simpson's term "intelligent love" or [novelist Henry] James's "emotional intelligence." Consider Mrs. Bennet's behavior upon learning that Lydia will be married, perhaps her most offensive display in the whole novel.

> It was a fortnight since Mrs. Bennet had been downstairs, but on this happy day, she again took her seat at the head of her table, and in spirits oppressively high. No sentiment of shame gave damp to her triumph. The marriage of a daughter, which had been the first object of her wishes, since Jane was sixteen, was now on the point of accomplishment, and her thoughts and her words ran wholly on those attendants of elegant nuptials, fine muslins, new carriages, and servants. She was busily searching through the neighborhood for a proper situation for her daughter, and, without knowing or considering what their income might be, rejected many as deficient in size and importance.

When, however, Mr. Bennet reveals to her "amazement and horror" that he will not advance a guinea to buy clothes for his daughter, Mrs. Bennet's astonishment knows no bounds. In a manner characteristic of Austen's narrative technique, the final sentence of the paragraph identifies the moral problem that the paragraph has been examining: "That his anger could be carried to such a point of inconceivable resentment, as to refuse his daughter a privilege, without which her marriage would scarcely seem valid, exceeded all that she could believe possible. She was more alive to the disgrace, which the want of new clothes must reflect on her

daughter's nuptials, than to any sense of shame at her eloping and living with Wickham, a fortnight before that took
place". Unable to distinguish significant from insignificant
experience, Mrs. Bennet can never see below the surface
and views, for example, Mr. Gardiner's sacrifices on behalf
of her daughter as an early Christmas present.

TOGETHER MRS. BENNET, LYDIA, AND MR. COLLINS CREATE IRRATIONALITY

The shamelessness of Mrs. Bennet's response is both an intellectual and a moral failing. Lydia, educated and admired
by her mother, is the best example of Austen's understanding of ingratitude. . . . Lydia's behavior at the Gardiners'
house in London at the time of her wedding exemplifies her
shamelessness. While she is dressing for the ceremony, Mrs.
Gardiner is trying to impress upon her some consciousness
of her actions. Lydia says, "However I did not hear above one
word in ten, for I was thinking, you may suppose, of my dear
Wickham. I longed to know whether he was wearing his
blue coat". In another situation the preoccupation with the
blue coat would be humorous; here, because it brings to
mind Mrs. Gardiner's painful version of the story, it only sig-
nifies the waste of suffering and effort behind the event
about to take place. Lydia's blindness is a matter of both the
mind and the heart. In her letter of elopement to Mrs.
Forster—"My Dear Harriet, You will laugh when you know
where I am gone"—she reveals a numbness of perception as
well as of feeling.

An important technique of moral comment, and certainly
of comedy, is the suggestion or juxtaposition of antithetical
experiences. When Mrs. Bennet equates Jane's face with the
fat haunch of venison as two things that must impress Bingley about her table, an almost metaphorical effect results, an
effect that Austen's novels are frequently said to lack. Mr.
Collins's equations are even more astonishing; when he
learns that the eldest Bennet daughter is engaged, he ac-
commodates himself: "Mr. Collins had only to change from
Jane to Elizabeth—and it was soon done—done while Mrs.
Bennet was stirring the fire". As Collins himself admits, the
choice of wife is the selection of another player at the
quadrille table at Rosings. Yet the humor of this mentality is
often qualified by a recognition of its danger. Upon Lydia's
elopement Mr. Collins makes an extraordinary comparison:

"The death of your daughter would have been a blessing in comparison of this". Here Mr. Collins's insensibility is instructive, for it reminds us that the event is not tragic, and it forces us to readopt the perspective we may have lost through sympathizing with Elizabeth.

The many outlandish equations in the speech of Mrs. Bennet, Mr. Collins, and Lydia create a powerful force of irrationality in the novel. Such bizarre juxtapositions have a way of neutralizing the whole experience of life. It is their impoverishing, indiscriminate strength that Darcy resists through his intellectual fastidiousness and temperamental rigidity. . . .

ELIZABETH AND DARCY ADOPT AN ADULT POSTURE TOWARD THE WORLD

All the men and women of Elizabeth's generation are actively involved in adopting their permanent, adult posture toward the world. The decisions and choices of the insensitive or unintelligent characters—Charlotte, Mr. Collins, Wickham, Lydia—are revealed in the way they view the selection of spouse: as a relatively uncomplicated decision, a matter of ambition or necessity. To the intelligent and sensitive person, like Elizabeth or Darcy, the choice of adult posture, like the choice of spouse, is most complex. To a person gifted with "emotional intelligence" in Jane Austen's world, the choice of moral stance in a world that is continually fluctuating under the active energies of sense and nonsense is as problematic as the individual's consciousness will allow. In *Pride and Prejudice* we view a variety of responses: Darcy, who is totally rigid in his refusal to give way to the exigencies of absurdity; Mr. Bennet, who capitulates entirely; Lady Catherine, who exemplifies what her nephew is in danger of becoming; and Elizabeth, who is susceptible to her father's chosen stance. Darcy must learn to laugh at himself and to develop a more generous attitude toward the absurdity of others. Elizabeth is the agent of this change, who has learned the value of laughter from her father, but who, under Darcy's influence, will not give in to it entirely. . . .

If, like Darcy, we separate ourselves from the anarchic elements of life, we must separate ourselves from the pleasures of expression altogether. It is as though every Elizabeth comes with a Mrs. Bennet, and you cannot have one without the other: in the words of T.S. Eliot, they are a "necessary conjunction." Darcy resists his attraction to Elizabeth in the beginning in part because he cannot tolerate her mother's anarchic vulgarity. Their marriage represents his capitulation to the force of irrationality as it does her surrender to the need for rationality. . . .

In selecting one another, Elizabeth and Darcy counteract the influences of their parents (in Darcy's case, his surrogate parent) and set forth on an improved project for the present, which is to say, the future. Like the perception of space, the perception of time in *Pride and Prejudice* is defined internally. Literal time is a few months, just long enough for the marriageable persons to court and marry. Internal time covers the psychic distance of three generations through exposing the actions of the central generation. The past and future do not exist as mysterious abysses; Austen's time is an eternal present, which encloses in its immediate alterations both the past and future. The individual is determined by his past, yet the very existence of this influence ensures the power of his will to affect the next generation. For this reason the choice of mate is the crucial act of life in *Pride and Prejudice*, the one most capable of effecting change and justifying hope. . . .

In Jane Austen, one generation is an eternity. What we do now is affected by what our parents did and will affect what our children do. This is the sum of what Elizabeth learns in her passage into adulthood. Only when she understands the extent of her own conditioning is she capable of transcending it: "[Elizabeth] had never felt so strongly as now, the disadvantages which must attend the children of so unsuitable a marriage". Her self-knowledge is solidly linked to a knowledge of her past and her family; not until she sees the past borne out in Lydia's fate does she become fully conscious of herself and capable of love.

Questioning the Merit of *Pride and Prejudice*

Roger Gard

Roger Gard invents an informal debate to examine *Pride and Prejudice.* The fictitious Henry and Alec, who consider a range of perspectives from traditional critics to modern feminists, discuss the merit of Austen's themes, characters, realism, and skill in comic art. Gard is a French author of plays and novels, including 'Emma' *and* 'Persuasion' and an eight-part novel, *Les Thebault.* He was awarded the Nobel Prize in literature in 1937.

I shall try to pay tribute to the ease of Jane Austen's most popular novel, and her favourite, by a variation in critical form. . . . The idea is of a lightly dramatised talk about books—or, literally, 'book-chat' (Gore Vidal's generic name for literary criticism). . . . I think there is a place and a use for a voice that can be sceptical of those simple assumptions of significance and *importance* that we tend to bring automatically to classic novels; and that has even the liberty to be Philistine—though not uneducated. Such a voice is, naturally, rarely present in books on Jane Austen. . . . Naturally there must also be a voice which answers. For convenience both are allowed to quote with unnaturistic accuracy, and at large: the questioner is called Alec, and the answerer, or defender, Henry. And this being to some extent a conversion narrative, the former will be heard mostly at first, and later mostly the latter. . . .

IS AUSTEN GREAT OR MERELY POPULAR?

Henry Jane Austen's popularity? You doubt whether so bright and easily available a comedy can be really great Art—art even in the same class as Shakespeare and Homer and Dante and Goethe and so on? World-historical art? Well, I won't insult you with the obvious arguments that intelligence and memorability and depth clearly don't require grandeur or breadth of subject—the latter in fact often go with stupid and superficial work. Breadth of *appeal* in both time and space is a different matter, and here impressions and gossip suggest part of an answer—I'm told, for instance, that in Bulgaria in the mid-1980s the State publishing house's issue of a translation of *Pride and Prejudice* vanished within a week or two—100,000 copies and only so relatively few because they hadn't paper to print more. Apparently these Bulgars liked the story. It makes one think. . . . But the more serious and substantial answers to your objections are to be got only by looking closely at what Jane Austen's comedy is *for*—at the ends encompassed by what you think merely a light amusement. I find that in its peculiarly vivid way this book shows, among other things, that the qualifications requisite for satisfactory marital relations, and thus for the maintenance of the health of the society to which they are central, are as much, if not more than, intellectual and spiritual as they are physical. A not unimportant matter surely? Observe in the first chapter . . .

Alec   How pompous this is! Of course such ideas are made clear as day by your novelist. One of her great virtues, so obvious that nobody seems to mention it, is the absence of blurred focus or double and contradictory meanings—ambiguity and all that. But does this encourage a profound vision or a vision relevant to us now? I fear that your Bulgarians wanted to escape into a fresher fantasy world, as remote as possible from shortages and politics and the twentieth century! As to what is 'said':—If I wanted to be entertained by little English moral commonplaces *naked*, as it were, I'd go to a philosopher or an essayist—even a sociologist. . . . But where I wouldn't look is in this very expert and cosy comic art. Moral sentiments just happen to be part of the raw material for clever novels of that period.

Is *Pride and Prejudice* Profound or Trivial?

Henry   What matters is the force and quality of the moral ideas.

Alec   Isn't that just the trouble?—they're simply impeccable—and therefore easy, comfortable and unexciting. Nobody *could* disagree with, let alone be disconcerted or challenged by, all this sensible decorous correct stuff about the desirable relations between the sexes. You want to take Austen as a didactic writer—or if not consciously that, some-one from whom one may learn lessons. Well, they're rather boring lessons. . . . We mustn't universalise anything more than ten years old in case we hurt their [contemporary crit-ics] timid relativism. Boring too, to people like me who care about the real world, because . . .

Henry   The real world, hum. Well . . .

Alec   Because you could derive the same ideas, *precisely* the same mark you, from lesser figures.[1] . . . I've noticed that even distinguished readers, professors at ancient universi-ties, find themselves—when talking about Austen's ideas—or the 'ideology' they deduce from the novels coming in a rush of frankness near to admitting that she is not, after all, so very great an artist! . . . Just snugly sitting there at the cen-tre, writing highly skilled little comedies . . . ? Well it might after all be as well to settle for that. There'd still be a grate-ful public. . . .

Consider the central illusion of supposedly realistic fiction—that it's a reflection of, and on, everyday life, like Stendhal's[2] travelling mirror. Life organised and pointed up perhaps, but none the less the kind of thing that prompts a traditionalist like you to prose on about virtuous marriages, or a feminist—who is the obverse of the same moralising coin actually. . . . You both take too much for granted. In this book life is so conven-tionalised and so patly put as to have no relation, no ex-ploratory relation at any rate, to any conceivable real.

Henry   It's difficult to counter such sweeping assertion, as you know. But I'll try. Look at the terms in which the novel is praised. It's wonderfully comic—and entertains the Bulgarians. Very well. But it's possible to be too much de-lighted with that, and miss the true, unique, distinction. This begins with the observation that the structure of *Pride and Prejudice* is so clearly articulated and cleverly played against *conventional* expectations about love stories that at least two strange and original effects are taken in by any reader with-out the least difficulty: first, the dynamic of love is based on initial disconcertment, dislike and embarrassment instead of the commonplace melting moods, so that obstacles are psychological and internal, not a matter of external bars. . . .

1. novelists of Jane Austen's time 2. pseudonym for Henri Beyle, one of the greatest of French novelists, known for his objective, dispassionate analysis of complicated states of consciousness

Alec   Very true. No one denies that it's a brilliantly written comedy. But so much of what you've said is about *art*—words, technique and the necessarily generalised and metaphorical notion of structure. I grant all this—but I still want to be convinced that this is a novel about serious issues. The conventions that you say Austen is so innovative about and with are predominantly the conventions of novel writing—polite female novel writing at that. The insight about falling in love might occur in any number of romantic stories.

HOW DO FEMINISTS VIEW *PRIDE AND PREJUDICE*?

Henry   Ah, yes, it's interesting that people who attack Jane Austen almost always merely dogmatise usually, to do feminists justice, from a snottily male point of view. . . . Yet it's exactly the modern female point of view that might interest you. It's true that you hear some feminists nowadays saying that it's our, or their, first duty as responsible readers to be alert to the primacy of pleasure—the *jouissance*[3] inherent in the play of signifiers. But they also argue that a lot of the interest of Jane Austen's work lies in what it says—or rather in what it can yield when its basic assumptions are called into question— examined—about early-ish capitalist power structures. Thus you can argue that Elizabeth seems to be able to win against her father and against Darcy only by manoeuvering within a system—a discourse—that inevitably privileges the male— who is, well, the controller of the means of production and exchange, isn't he? Accordingly, who could fail to notice the prominence accorded, in the revaluation of Darcy within the novel, to his character as a good patriarch? . . . And who, by contrast, could fail to notice that much of the irresponsibility of Mr. Bennet himself is comprised in his failure (like that of Austen's own father it is sometimes hazarded, though unfairly and anachronistically) to supply the wherewithal for a marriage in that society—a large dowry? . . .

The only problem with this is that the more extreme feminists seem unsure as to whether Jane Austen herself was sufficiently conscious of this, which I'm confident she was. But otherwise it's an argument that seems to me both true and powerful. Is that serious enough for you?

Alec   The last point is the most interesting. How can we tell how conscious the comic moralist is of what can be in-

3. enjoyment

ferred from her works when we dethrone intention and treat them as *documents*? . . . My real point is that most of your argument, like most of what you said earlier, may well be true but, as the terms used to describe it suggest, it doesn't require a *novel* to say it in. In fact, the charm and success of the dramatisation may get in the way, may distract and blur and sugar such cutting analyses. To be candid, it's a point that ought to be made about a lot of novels, not just *Pride and Prejudice*. They are entertainments *primarily*. . . . The materials, and the morals, are commonplace—though Austen is never less than intelligent. What is distinct and fun is the way she is handles things . . .

Henry   I'm amazed how confusing this really somewhat elementary subject can become. Is it beneath you to descend into the specific?—people make such a virtue of the high abstract these days.

ARE THE CHARACTERS FRESH OR PREDICTABLE?

Alec   I'd be glad to. Let's sample the texture of the novel. . . . The action around the central consciousness—Elizabeth—is typically a matter of stock responses which are evinced with

A MODERN CRITIC'S ENDORSEMENT

In her 1939 book, Jane Austen and Her Art, *Mary Lascelles praises Austen's charm and her ability to invite readers into her work, as if the author were a friend.*

What distinguishes Jane Austen's manner of inviting us to share in the act of creation but a greater delicacy of intimation? Her invitation is not conveyed directly at any given moment—when it might be summarily refused. It is implicit in all her dealings with us, in what [Walter] Raleigh called 'a certain subtle literary politeness that is charm itself' above all in her mood of hospitality. 'The truth is,' [short-story writer] Katherine Mansfield writes, 'that every true admirer of the novels cherishes the happy thought that he alone—reading between the lines—has become the secret friend of their author.' How has it come about that we feel so towards this most reserved of writers? That very reticence may suggest a partial explanation: '. . . the personality of the author,' [novelist] Henry James says, '. . . however enchanting, is a thing for the reader only, and not for the author himself . . . to count in at all.'

Mary Lascelles, *Jane Austen and Her Art.* 1939. Reprint, London: Oxford University Press, 1963.

that kind of predictability that tells us very little indeed new about the human soul—but a lot about comic effects. The figures whose moral and spiritual welfare—and even social and political implications—you profess to learn from or about are stereotypes who delight us by reacting regularly— even oppressively so—to a flat pattern. . . .

Consider a typical situation near the beginning, in chapter seven—Jane has received a letter and Mrs. Bennet says "Well, Jane, who is it from? what is it about? what does he say? Well, Jane make haste and tell us. . . ." Anyway, the letter turns out to be from Miss Bingley asking Jane to dine because—this is the point—her brother won't be there, and "the gentlemen are to dine with the officers". Hark what discord follows:

> "With the officers!" cried Lydia. "I wonder my aunt did not tell us of *that.*"
> "Dining out," said Mrs. Bennet, "that is very unlucky."
> "Can I have the carriage?" said Jane.
> "No, my dear, you had better go on horseback, because it seems likely to rain; then you must stay all night."
> "That would be a good scheme," said Elizabeth, "if you were sure they would not offer to send her home."
> "Oh! but the gentlemen will have Mr. Bingley's chaise to go to Meryton; and the Hursts have no horses to theirs."
> "I had much rather go in the coach."
> "But, my dear, your father cannot spare the horses, I am sure, they are wanted in the farm, Mr. Bennet, are not they?"
> "They are wanted in the farm much oftener than I can get them."
> "But if you have got them to day," said Elizabeth, "my mother's purpose will be answered."
> She did at last extort from her father an acknowledgement that the horses were engaged. Jane was therefore obliged to go on horseback, and her mother attended her to the door with many cheerful prognostics of a bad day.

Terrific. This isn't a highlight or a great set piece as it might be in a lesser author: it's part of the ordinary stuff of the book. But it'd be just puffery and bad faith—and an offence against decorum and the law of kinds—to claim to see in it great psychological insight. "People are trapped in their characteristics. They act parts.". . . Writers are said to be capable of killing for a joke, and I believe it.

Henry But the jokes are brilliant serious jokes—about moral qualities or their absence. I don't see what you're claiming here.

Alec I'm claiming to be faithful to what Austen really offers as opposed to what you want her to offer. . . . What distinguishes Austen is her speed coupled with what I expect some of your marxising feminists would call the essential conservatism of a practice through which entirely predictable effects about entirely predictable moral attitudes are secured and enjoyed. The *point* is the predictability. We don't want to learn anything new. So: Lydia catches at any mention of officers; Jane doesn't want to presume on staying the night and getting a chance of seeing Bingley; Mrs. Bennet wants the weather and *no* carriage, to make sure that she does; Elizabeth is amused and wants to expose these subterranean meanings; Mr. Bennet embraces a chance to be sardonic about his family. . . .

It's a kind of principle with these novelists that all their figures inevitably *speak up* consistently. It's just as bare as *Sense and Sensibility* here—like a mechanism, a chiming clock—and so far from the lively untidiness of real existence as to rule out any but the charming, light, effects of Art. The implied author, and her collaborator, the reader, are always too right, according to their little code, to allow in the breath of life. . . . In this book the morality is too pat, almost complacent. And, really, it's the morality of a past age and a limited society. So tiny and insular that I'm amused at the antics; touched by the consummately judged little love story—but for any breadth and passion I go elsewhere! . . .

Henry   All I feel is that you agree that Jane Austen is writing in a convention. What does your demand for passion or grandeur amount to? Must one be always meditating Michaelangelo on the Capitol? Perhaps you're one of those readers who only recognises seriousness when it appears in conscious and semi-clerical dress. But in my opinion you appreciate no art at all if you appreciate *all* art in a solemn or grandiose sort of way. As to "provincial", everything is rooted somewhere, and life is as real in Hampshire and Surrey[4] as it ever was in St. Petersburg or Elsinore.[5]

---

4. areas where Jane Austen lived   5. i.e., settings of Tolstoy or Shakespeare's masterpieces

CHAPTER 4

Symbol and Language

READINGS ON
PRIDE AND PREJUDICE

The Significance of Gardens and Pastoral Scenes

Alison G. Sulloway

Alison G. Sulloway analyzes Austen's use of garden settings and pastoral scenes. Besides generally using gardens as places of personal comfort and freedom for both men and women, Austen uses Pemberley and two other pastoral settings in particular for Elizabeth and Darcy to communicate their affections and reconcile their differences. Alison G. Sulloway taught English at Columbia University, Beloit College, and Virginia Polytechnic Institute and State University. She is the author of *Gerard Manley Hopkins and the Victorian Temper,* and "Emma Woodhouse and a *Vindication of the Rights of Women".*

Because orthodox writers on "the woman question" were obsessed with Milton's Eve[1] and with the archetypal female sinner in Genesis, they were equally obsessed with contemporary women in gardens. The garden symbolized the utmost theoretical extension of a young unmarried woman's province, where she could be alone outdoors with no loss of safety or propriety. . . .

Austen's primary responses to gardens and pastoral scenes in her fiction and her letters differed profoundly from those of orthodox males. She simply loved them for themselves, for their beauty and the invigorating support that they offered to people under stress, and for the archetypal reassurances they provided, as budding, blooming, or falling leaves and flowers responded to the cycle of the seasons.

But discreet symbolist that Austen was, she also loved pastoral scenes for patriotic reasons. Napoleon had been

1. the biblical Eve in John Milton's poem *Paradise Lost*

threatening to make England's gardens and pastures his property, as though the country for which Austen's naval brothers were fighting was a mere woman, ripe for his exploitation. Austen had seen and suffered enough casual exploitation so that she took the pastoral world under her tender but unobtrusive fictional protection, just as she felt protective toward human figures under threat of abuse or neglect. . . .

GARDENS SYMBOLIZE MALE-FEMALE ROLES

Austen was very well aware, as well, that gardens symbolized not only those pastoral pleasures that could unite men and women on plantations, but also all the patriarchal arrangements that divided the two sexes. Marion Morrison[2] has drawn a delightful picture of the proprietorial male's pleasure in his gardens as it appears in Austen's fiction. Although the plantation gardens signify in part all the privileges that supported men's dominion over women, the more admirable male characters knew that women's welfare on an estate depended entirely on the managerial efficiency of its owner, and on his willingness to let her share in its benefits without crippling restrictions.

> We watch the country gentlemen and their visitors surveying happily their groves and coppices, their lime walk, their stretch of water, their ha-ha,[3] their prospects and vistas, dovecotes,[4] stewponds, and succession houses. Mr. Bennet escapes to the little copse at Longbourn; Mr. Woodhouse [in *Emma*], warmly wrapped, walks in the shrubbery at Harfield; Colonel Brandon [in *Sense and Sensibility*], in his flannel waistcoat, is ensconced in the yew arbor at Delaford; the Musgrove children [in *Persuasion*] play on the lawn at Uppercross. Familiar "props" appear again and again; the plantation, the summer house or arbor bower (sometimes damp), the gravel walk, the sweep, the paddock, and above all, the shrubbery.

The shrubbery was important because young unmarried women—the elder Bennet sisters and Fanny Price [in *Mansfield Park*], for instance—often escape there for privacy. But Morrison's charming paragraph and her whole short essay unconsciously dwells more upon the master's pride and ownership in each heroine's outdoor province, than in her welcome and comfortable presence there. . . .

Austen's heroines are unusually casual about leaving the estate alone, as provincial gentlewomen went—or ideally,

2. in "Gardens" in *The Jane Austen Companion* 3. a hedge serving as a fence 4. a structure on a pole for housing domestic pigeons

were not supposed to go. Catherine Morland [in *Northanger Abbey*], the Bennet sisters, the Dashwood sisters [in *Sense and Sensibility*], and Anne Elliot [in *Persuasion*] roam by themselves all over the countryside, yet they were not supposed to discuss the weather: Chapman[5] observes blandly that "the weather was another subject on which only masculine opinion was valued." And readers are all subliminally or otherwise aware that Austen was forced to tether all her heroines fairly close to the province of the home. . . .

Since for Austen, all orthodox prescriptions against healthy occupations smacked of that "Evangelical" temper that she had told [her sister] Cassandra she disliked, her heroines' conduct in gardens symbolized the extent to which they had or had not been mentally deformed by feminine protocols. Elizabeth Bennet and Jane not only dance with verve and pleasure, but they run eagerly toward each other after they have been separated, or run anxiously toward their lazy and irresponsible father, so as to quicken his lethargic disinclination to rescue the eloping Lydia. There is no false bodily languor in either of them, despite Jane's habit of psychological denials. Elizabeth's spontaneous act of leaping over stiles so as to arrive quickly at her sick sister's bedside eventually received Darcy's warm praise. . . .

But Austen knew that when a young woman lavishes affection over nature, however discreetly, as Fanny Price lavishes affection over the great panoply of the stars, and does so in Edmund Bertram's presence, she may continue to do so, as long as this topic meets with the man's approval, since to praise nature discreetly is to indicate to a lover that a woman understands her utterly subordinate place in it. For a woman to praise nature is thus a very discreet form of courtship. . . .

DARCY ON HIS ESTATE

To suggest that Austen's Darcy, as the "preserver" of Pemberley, is a genuine green-world lover, may seem at first to compound the difficulties inherent in the implausibly double-natured character of Darcy, the haughty masculine snob, and Darcy, the benevolent feudal squire, stereotypically redeemed by a good woman's love. Darcy is a product of the female imagination as it responds to its predicament in the easiest subconscious way it knows how—through wish fulfill-

5. biographer and critic R.W.

ment. . . . This tall, rich, handsome aristocrat is also what every man envies; he stalks through the land, legally beholden to nobody—he is an orphan and he has therefore already stepped into "Dead men's Shoes", as Pemberley's Henry V. Abroad, he acknowledges no social superiors and he submits to no constraints of courtesy or charity. His intellectual and social judgments are fallible, because he is too consumed with himself to judge reliably about others or for others, even assuming that he has the right to judge for others in the first place.

Darcy appeals to women because the fantasy of taming the male beast who is brutal or indifferent to woman's dignity is as old a fantasy as it is in vulnerable, dependent children, whose dreams and fantasies of psychic wounds miraculously healed, parents reconciled, and paradise otherwise regained, are now acknowledged archetypes.

How, then, does Austen make this impossible man palatable, and even aesthetically, or symbolically at least, believable to those who struggle along with the unredeemable Darcys every day of their lives? The answer is that he is really more comfortable outdoors, with horse and hounds, with rod and gun through brightest Pemberley, and with taxes and tenants, and in his free moments from administering the estate, he is much happier in his library than he is in the confines of female provinces, such as ballrooms and the drawing rooms, with their predictable shallow mothers and daughters on the prowl to ensnare him into a disastrous marriage. On his own estate he is legally and socially lord of all he surveys, and these series of reassuring patriarchal surroundings all allow him to function there as a sensible, responsible, serious, benevolent despot of the Hobbsian kind,[6] who will engage Elizabeth's affectionate humor, as well as her ardent respect.

The Pemberley scenes, which have transfixed generations of critics, accomplish Austen's aesthetic and ethical miracles, even though they perilously skirt stereotypes, and they do so triumphantly. Austen's alchemy is primarily mythical and symbolic. First, she invokes the spacious beauties of Pemberley, both the internal and external, which are to be her heroine's vastly extended spatial and mental provinces in the future, and then she deftly connects them not only

---

6. a political theory advocating absolute monarchy, a theory advanced by English political philosopher Thomas Hobbes

ELIZABETH UNEXPECTEDLY MEETS DARCY AT PEMBERLEY

In their surprise encounter amid the trees, walks, and hills of Pemberley, Darcy maintains his civility and courtesy, but Elizabeth, unsure of her role, blushes, thinking her admiration of the estate's beauty may be misinterpreted.

They pursued the accustomed circuit; which brought them again, after some time, in a descent among hanging woods, to the edge of the water, in one of its narrowest parts. They crossed it by a simple bridge, in character with the general air of the scene; it was a spot less adorned than any they had yet visited; and the valley, here contracted into a glen, allowed room only for the stream, and a narrow walk amidst the rough coppice-wood which bordered it. Elizabeth longed to explore its windings; but when they had crossed the bridge, and perceived their distance from the house, Mrs. Gardiner, who was not a great walker, could go no farther, and thought only of returning to the carriage as quickly as possible. Her niece was, therefore, obliged to submit, and they took their way towards the house on the opposite side of the river, in the nearest direction; but their progress was slow, for Mr. Gardiner, though seldom able to indulge the taste, was very fond of fishing, and was so much engaged in watching the occasional appearance of some trout in the water, and talking to the man about them, that he advanced but little. Whilst wandering on in this slow manner, they were again surprised, and Elizabeth's astonishment was quite equal to what it had been at first, by the sight of Mr. Darcy approaching them, and at no great distance. The walk being here less sheltered than on the other side, allowed them to see him before they met. Elizabeth, however astonished, was at least more prepared for an interview than before, and resolved to appear and to speak with calmness, if he really intended to meet them. For a few moments, indeed, she felt that he would probably strike into some other path. This idea lasted while a turning in the walk concealed him from their view; the turning past, he was immediately before them. With a glance she saw, that he had lost none of his recent civility; and, to imitate his politeness, she began, as they met, to admire the beauty of the place; but she had not got beyond the words "delightful," and "charming," when some unlucky recollections obtruded, and she fancied that praise of Pemberley from her, might be mischievously construed. Her colour changed, and she said no more.

Jane Austen, *Pride and Prejudice*

with the present owner's inherited and authoritative male role, but she also invokes his *pastoral* forbearance, in both senses of the reverberative adjective *pastoral.* He is the proverbial biblical "good steward," a good father, or a good shepherd or secular pastor to his inheritance under his care. And as his housekeeper implies, he is as good a secular shepherd to his tenants, his servants, and his surrogate-daughter, who is really his sister, the terrified young woman "*en Penitence,*" Georgiana Darcy. He is even singularly generous where Georgiana Darcy is concerned, for he knows that his treatment of her has been heavy-handed, especially since their father left him as her guardian. He welcomes the partnership of Elizabeth, who will be to Georgiana, indoors and out, a careful mentor of Georgiana's fullest possible autonomous development.

COMPARATIVE WORDS DETERMINE EMOTIONAL RESPONSE

Austen's secondary magical techniques are rhetorical, even grammatical, as well as symbolical and mythical. For as Elizabeth moves about Pemberley, looking at the fine scenes and vistas from the spacious interior as well as from the almost limitless plantations, and as she acknowledges with longing what she now supposes she has lost, Austen's indirectly authorial voice—half hers and half Elizabeth's, which extols Pemberley's domestic beauties and its woods, fields, hills, valleys, pastures, and trout streams—moves from the mere positive grammatical degree, in which beautiful scenes and their accompanying fine ethical values appear merely *very* beautiful indeed, and then later to the comparative degree, where they appear even *more beautiful yet.* But about the owner of this earthly paradise, only the superlative degree will do: he is the *finest* landlord imaginable.

> First, every disposition of the ground was good; and she looked on the whole scene, the river, the trees scattered on its bands, and the winding of the valley as far as she could trace it, with delight. As they passed into the other rooms, these objects were taking different positions; but from every window there were beauties to be seen. The rooms were lofty and handsome, and their furniture suitable to the fortune of their proprietor; but Elizabeth saw, with the admiration of his taste, that it was neither gaudy nor uselessly fine; with less of splendor, and more of real elegance, than the furniture of Rosings.

Darcy's housekeeper speaks of him in the superlative; "He is the best landlord, and the best master . . . that ever lived. Not like the wild young men now-a-days, who think of nothing but themselves." Readers' minds will inevitably contrast this patriarchal paragon with John Dashwood, the reckless hacker of his father's fine timber, or Tom Bertram [in *Mansfield Park*], the prodigal son, wasting his father's substance on England's racecourses, or Sir Walter Elliot [in *Persuasion*], who thinks only of the social prestige that his estate bestows upon him, and not what he owes to it and to its dependent female residents.

When Elizabeth has had her fill of all these domestic and pastoral beauties, "they walked across the lawn towards the river," and she "turned back to look again; her uncle and aunt stopped also, and while the former was conjecturing as to the date of the building, the owner of it himself suddenly came forward from the road, which led behind it to the stables." This abrupt arrival of "the owner himself" might well suggest something of the providential about it. In any case, there is something profoundly moving in the fact that Elizabeth has courageously allowed herself to spend time mourning what she supposed herself to have lost; she does so now without any sycophantic gratitude to Darcy, merely a frank and honest acknowledgment of the serious and important role she could have played as Pemberley's mistress.

Elizabeth's mourning is fully as much ethical as economic and aesthetic. Expanded ethical and functional opportunities would indeed, she assumes, have been hers. Instead of having to pander to a contemptuous father and a neurotic mother, she would have been offered an administrative post worthy of her conscience and her talents. But because she is willing to go through a painful process, which in modern psychology is beginning to be known as "the work of mourning," and to endure the final pain of her last look at her lost paradise, she gains it. The owner returns, and paradise may yet be hers.

After Darcy has spoken most courteously to her and to her beloved aunt and uncle, despite his embarrassment, and after he has engaged them for visits the next day, Elizabeth and the Gardiners tactfully leave "the present owner" to his magnificent estate. But now it is not merely beautiful in every way to Elizabeth; it is even *more* beautiful than she had previously thought, since shock has quickened her perceptions: "They had now entered a beautiful walk by the side of the water, and every step was bringing forward a *nobler* fall of ground, or a *finer* reach of the woods to which they were approaching; but it was some time before Elizabeth was sensible of any of it" (emphasis mine).

Elizabeth's mind is only intermittently upon these beauties so glowingly described in this monologue, half hers and half authorial. The other half of Elizabeth's mind yearns to know exactly what spot inside Pemberley its owner now graces. This scene represents one of those rare moments in Austen's fiction when a woman is actually observed standing outside, in her exile, debarred now from entering a privileged house of beauty and plenty, and condemned, she supposes, to return to a house of resentful parents and three shallow, bad-tempered sisters. Austen's scenic recognition of women's double jeopardy, incarceration or exile, is more likely to occur in scenes where women watch the men from garden plots or from windows, while these emancipated creatures come and go on foot or on horseback, upon their own freely chosen pursuits.

Austen's subtle grammatical distinctions between the positive degree—"large, handsome stone building" flanked by the "natural beauty of the setting"—and the superlative degree, with its sensation of a crescendo at its height, as the housekeeper describes the master of all these beauties in the superlative degree—"the best landlord, the finest master"—and then the falling sense of tumescence,[7] in the mere comparative degree of exterior beauties, as in "a nobler fall of ground or a finer reach of woods," all suggest the symbolic postcoital *tristesse*[8] that Elizabeth is now enduring. Austen's skillful management of grammatical forms symbolizing emotions that she was not allowed to express or even to know about as an unmarried woman, should have prevented all critical stereotypes about the sexless Miss Austen.

LOVERS RECONCILED IN PASTORAL SETTING

There is another fine pastoral scene, or rather two of them, when Elizabeth and Darcy achieve the reconciliation of lovers that is comparable to no other. Darcy, now free of all his false pride and prejudices, and Elizabeth now quickly freeing herself of the prickly defensiveness into which his insults have driven her, wander together over and beyond the boundaries of Longbourn plantation, having no idea how far they have gone or how long they have been out together. During both

7. a swelling or enlarging 8. sadness; sorrow

these scenes, Darcy does penance in a manner customarily thought necessary only for the female sex:

> As a child I was taught what was *right*, but left to follow right conduct in pride and conceit. Unfortunately an only son, (for many years an only *child*), I was spoilt by my parents, who though good in themselves . . . allowed, encouraged, even taught me to be selfish and overbearing, to care for none beyond my own family circle, to think meanly of all the rest of the world, to *wish* at least to think meanly of their sense and worth compared to my own.

Darcy's monologue to Elizabeth, which goes on for one whole page, contains many phrases by which feminists had earlier made their charges against the male sex: "spoilt," "selfish," "overbearing," "taught to think meanly of [women's] sense and worth compared to [their] own" are accusations that could be found in almost any radical or moderate feminist tract. Elizabeth then comforts Darcy by reminding him that the "conduct of neither, if strictly examined, will be irreproachable," as indeed, hers has not been according either to contemporary or to modern orthodoxies about proper conduct in women. She is now too tactful to remind him that he had earlier provided her with endless "provocations" and that she had "some excuse for incivility if [she] *was* uncivil." Now she acknowledges her mistake about Wickham, but she will not grovel even before the man she has won, and even as she earlier had grovelled in private, according to orthodox dictates about the immense and life-long gratitude that a woman in love owed to the man who had stooped to make her his wife.

Now the lovers' reconciliation is complete; and Elizabeth can lighten Darcy's profound sense of guilt with gentle wit—but not at his expense. They now wander on together, discussing the best ways to smooth over the relations between their adversarial families. As Austen said in another connection with another pair of reconciling lovers, most of us know where we are and what time it is during the passing hours, "yet with lovers it is different. Between *them* no subject is finished, no communication is even made, till it had been made at least twenty times over." Nowhere is the sense of Austenian context sharper than in Austen's pastoral scenes.

Letters in *Pride and Prejudice*

Lloyd W. Brown

Lloyd W. Brown argues that in addition to their function as important extensions of conversation, letters add other dimensions to plot and theme in Austen's novels, particularly in *Pride and Prejudice.* Brown identifies four purposes of Austen's letter writing: to disseminate facts, to reveal personal values and feelings, to incorporate themes, and to dramatize turning points. Darcy's letter to Elizabeth after their quarrel incorporates all four purposes. Lloyd W. Brown is the author of the journal articles "The Comic Conclusion in Jane Austen's Novels" and "Jane Austen and the Sublime: A Note on *Mansfield Park*," and *The Black Writer in Africa and the Americas* and *West Indian Poetry.*

In a letter to her sister Cassandra, Jane Austen observes, "I have now attained the true art of letter-writing, which we are always told, is to express on paper exactly what one would say to the same person by word of mouth; I have been talking to you almost as fast as I could the whole of this letter" (*Letters*). As usual, Jane Austen's flippant tone fails to disguise the seriousness of her literary judgment, for the remark really demonstrates her interest in the letter as an extension of conversation. The true art of letter writing is analogous to the polite traditions of conversation. This parallel is crucial to an understanding of the function of letters in her fiction. Occasionally, Jane Austen's personal correspondence notes the importance of letters in the straightforward dissemination of facts (*Letters*); and this role is fairly evident in the novels. Mr. Collins' visit to Longbourn is heralded by his letter to Mr. Bennet. . . .

But as Jane Austen's own comparison of letter writing

with conversation makes clear, she is more interested in letters (in fiction and in real life) as the direct transmission of personal values and feeling. In essence, epistolary styles are as integral to the theme and structure of each work as individual conversation. . . .

Like her views on conversation, Jane Austen's concept of epistolary self-revelation is comparable with those of her eighteenth-century predecessors, especially Samuel Richardson. In *Clarissa* there are several reminders of Richardson's faith in the letter as a kind of confessional. This belief is voiced by Belford who asserts that the style of those "writing of and in the midst of *present* distresses is *much more* lively and affecting" than the "dry" and "unanimated" narrative that describes "dangers surmounted.". . .

In effect, the writing of a letter is at once an act of confession and an experience in conflict. The writer's instinct to project a favorable image of himself is counteracted by the letter's inherent tendency to be self-expressive. The process of spontaneous self-revelation is not wholly negated by deliberate efforts at concealment—it is simply transformed into unconscious self-betrayal. . . .

Jane Austen's treatment of epistolary styles attests to her awareness of these psychological subtleties. Her emphasis on the self-expressiveness of Fanny Knight's letters[1] is matched by her exploitation of epistolary styles, in the novels, as the means of unintended self-betrayal. Hence the irony of Mr. Collins' self-conscious style, both as a letter writer and as a conversationalist, lies in the fact that his native stupidity is repeatedly dramatized by the very orotundity that is meant to demonstrate intelligence. . . . These "confessional" and self-betraying functions which Jane Austen's fictional letters inherit from Richardson do not exhaust the potential of epistolary forms in her novels. The third role, which Richardson also develops, is quite as important. Specifically, the letter writer not only engages in some kind of self-portrayal, but he also contributes his style and judgment to the presentation of other characters. . . .

AUSTEN USES EPISTOLARY TECHNIQUES TO INCORPORATE THEMES

Jane Austen's early achievement in integrating moral psychology with the epistolary process is not really diminished by the

---

1. Jane Austen corresponded with her niece Fanny Knight.

fact that she abandons the letter-writing structure in *Lady Susan* and in subsequent novels. The "straight" narrative on which she concentrates from here on obviously provides the detached perspective that is essential to the play of satiric comment, and to the ironic shifts of narrative viewpoint. . . .

Thus the facility with which Jane Austen integrates certain themes with her narrative form, in subsequent novels, can be traced to her early education in epistolary fiction. This is particularly true of *Pride and Prejudice* and *Emma*. In each work Jane Austen draws upon her early experience with epistolary techniques in order to incorporate the themes of prejudice and imagination within her narrative structure. Hence the presentation of character and incident through the prejudices of Elizabeth Bennet and Emma Woodhouse is based on the same strategy that Richardson uses in depicting Solmes, or which Jane Austen herself utilizes in portraying Mr. Watts in *Three Sisters*. The initial portrait of Darcy, for example, depends largely on the prejudiced judgments of Elizabeth and Wickham. . . . The "real" Darcy only begins to emerge in *Pride and Prejudice* after Elizabeth collates a variety of personal judgments, including Darcy's own self-appraisal. . . .

LETTERS DRAMATIZE TURNING POINTS

To this perspectival role we must add the emotive functions of the epistolary mode in Jane Austen's mature narrative. The writing or the reading of letters is almost invariably crucial to the dramatic and psychological development of plot and character. Jane Austen exploits the inherent emotional values of the letter-writing process, and it probably accounts for the fact that so few of the letters in the novels are obscure or easily forgotten. Letter writing coincides with, and represents, the dramatic intensification of emotional and moral conflicts: Darcy's letter to Elizabeth Bennet, Lady Bertram's news of Mansfield Park crises, or Captain Wentworth's explosive proposal of marriage to Anne Elliot. And letters may either report or precipitate a crisis. Mr. Collins' visit to Longbourn is announced by letter; and so are the details of Lydia Bennet's elopement. Whether they are factual reports or personal self-expression, these letters are timed to dramatize the crucial turning points of narrative and theme. But the dramatic impact of many messages is derived from their emotional expressiveness. . . .

It is this sense of dramatic timing and emotional interaction that enables Jane Austen to derive maximum effects from a rather economical use of letters. In *Northanger Abbey* only two letters are quoted at length. But because of their precise timing they interact with, and become integral to, the most critical moments of Catherine Morland's development. . . .

LETTERS IN *PRIDE AND PREJUDICE* TIMED FOR DRAMATIC IMPACT

There are far more numerous letters in *Pride and Prejudice*, but generally, they too are timed for the same degree of dramatic impact that is achieved by the more limited correspondence of *Northanger Abbey*. All the crucial facts of Lydia's elopement are related by letters from Jane Bennet and the Gardiners. And in her crudely light-hearted way even Lydia is aware of the dramatic potential of the letter in her affair. As she advises Harriet Foster, "You need not send them word at Longbourn of my going, if you do not like it, for it will make the surprise the greater, when I write to them, and sign my name Lydia Wickham. What a good joke it will be! I can hardly write for laughing". Even the fairly routine incident of Mr. Collins' first letter to Longbourn has dramatic functions that go beyond the self-exposure of the writer's absurdities. As usual Jane Austen has concentrated on the reaction to the letter, and in so doing has transformed Mr. Collins' note into a touchstone for the self-revelation of the readers. Elizabeth's quick-witted common sense is exemplified by her finding that Mr. Collins "must be an oddity" with "something very pompous in his stile." Her father's opinion confirms the similarity of their tastes: "There is a mixture of servility and self-importance in his letter, which promises well." Mary demonstrates her own pomposity by praising Mr. Collins' style, and neither Catherine nor Lydia is impressed with the matter: "It was next to impossible that their cousin should come in a scarlet coat, and it was now some weeks since they had received pleasure from the society of a man in any other colour".

The most crucial letter is, of course, the one written by Darcy after his quarrel with Elizabeth. Here, too, the dramatic function of the letter hinges on the emotional interaction of writer and reader. In one sense Darcy's choice of a letter as the means of explaining his past conduct conforms with realistic convention: it would be unnatural for a man of his reserve and sensitivity to make such intimate revelations in any other form. But it is equally significant that the medium of his choice epitomizes the primary impulse behind Darcy's wish to communicate with Elizabeth—the compulsive need for self-justification:

> Two offences of a very different nature, and by no means of equal magnitude, you last night laid to my charge. The first mentioned was, that, regardless of the sentiments of either, I had detached Mr. Bingley from your sister,—and the other, that I had, in defiance of various claims, in defiance of honour and humanity, ruined the immediate prosperity, and blasted the prospects of Mr. Wickham.—Wilfully and wantonly to have thrown off the companion of my youth, the acknowledged favourite of my father, a young man who had scarcely any other dependence than on our patronage, and who had been brought up to expect its exertion, would be a depravity, to which the separation of two young persons, whose affection could be the growth of only a few weeks, could bear no comparison.—But from the severity of that blame which was last night so liberally bestowed, respecting each circumstance, I shall hope to be in future secured, when the following account of my actions and their motives has been read.—If, in the explanation of them which is due to myself, I am under the necessity of relating feelings which may be offensive to your's, I can only say that I am sorry.—The necessity must be obeyed—and farther apology would be absurd.

It is appropriate that Darcy is sensitive to Elizabeth's possible reactions, for his letter does precipitate an emotional crisis which compels Elizabeth to readjust her perspectives. Jane Austen's faith in the emotive powers of the letter underlies Elizabeth's reception of Darcy's note. Moreover, the range of Elizabeth's responses supports Samuel Richardson's thesis on the arresting powers of correspondence. Here, for the first time, Darcy's character has been exposed in a form and context which frees Elizabeth's shaky judgment from the distracting clashes of debate, and from the kind of distorting conflicts that marked the Hunsford quarrel. The nature of Elizabeth's reaction to Darcy's newly revealed personality has been conditioned by his medium of communication. For now, unlike their personal meetings, she has the opportunity to reconsider initial responses. She can evaluate her prejudice in the light of Darcy's statements and attitudes, now that the epistolary form has literally made them accessible for reexamination. In other words, the epistolary mode is really a psychological opportunity for the only effective weapon against irrational prepossession—thoughtful revaluation.

DARCY'S LETTER CAUSES ELIZABETH TO THINK AND RECONSIDER

Her initial impressions are colored by the old prejudices, and therefore tend to be highly emotional. Darcy's letter excites "a contrariety of emotion":

> With amazement did she first understand that he believed any apology to be in his power; and stedfastly was she persuaded that he could have no explanation to give, which a just sense of shame would not conceal. With a strong prejudice against every thing he might say, she began his account of what had happened at Netherfield. She read with an eagerness which hardly left her power of comprehension, and from impatience of knowing what the next sentence might bring, and incapable of attending to the sense of the one before her eyes. His belief of her sister's insensibility, she instantly resolved to be false, and his account of the real, the worst objections to the match, made her too angry to have any wish of doing him justice. He expressed no regret for what he had done which satisfied her; his style was not penitent, but haughty. It was all pride and insolence.

Furthermore, Darcy's account of Wickham arouses feelings that "were yet more acutely painful and more difficult of definition. Astonishment, apprehension, and even horror, oppressed her." Generally, her first response to the letter is remarkably similar to the unreceptive obstinacy which had created a barrier of noncommunication on both sides: "She wished to discredit it entirely, repeatedly exclaiming, 'This must be false! This cannot be! This must be the grossest falsehood!'—and when she had gone through the whole letter, though scarcely knowing any thing of the last page or two, put it hastily away, protesting that she would not regard it, that she would never look in it again". But the letter, Darcy's personality under hand and seal, remains accessible for further scrutiny. It is "unfolded again" in half a minute. And the blind passion of her earlier, prejudiced reading has been replaced by a resolve to be rational: "collecting herself as well as she could, she again began the mortifying perusal of all that related to Wickham, and commanded herself so far as to examine the meaning of every sentence". Rational deliberation produces new impressions of Wickham, and leads in turn to an equally balanced rereading of Darcy's self-defense with regards to Jane and Bingley. She finally accepts Darcy's letter after "wandering along the lane for two hours, giving way to every variety of thought; reconsidering events, determining probabilities, and reconciling herself as well as she could, to a change so sudden and so important". The progression from blind "contrariety of emotion" to self-knowledge dramatically illustrates how ignorance and pre-possession give way to rational awareness in *Pride and Prejudice.* The emotive functions of the epistolary mode have conformed with the thematic directions of the novel. . . .

In *Pride and Prejudice,* Darcy's note makes Elizabeth acutely conscious of her family's embarrassing shortcomings, and subsequently, her mortification is intensified by Jane's news of Lydia's elopement. On the whole the ego-centric motives of correspondents in Jane Austen's novels exemplify her consistent ability to integrate the psychological experiences of the epistolary mode with her primary themes. On the basis of her knowledge of Richardson, and as a result of her own experiments in the juvenilia, Jane Austen's epistolary structures serve to dramatize emotional crises. Isabella's shallow excuses, Darcy's proud self-defense, and Frank Churchill's apologetics—these are all vital to the final resolution of psychological crises in *Northanger Abbey, Pride and Prejudice,* and *Emma,* respectively. And they have been aptly dramatized by the natural self-regard of each writer. Conversely, their impact depends in part on the equally egocentric interests of the letter reader. . . . The true art of letter writing is not simply a communicative technique. It is also a complex experience of feeling and insights, through which individual perception and human relationships are defined.

CHAPTER 5

Irony and Wit

READINGS ON
PRIDE AND PREJUDICE

Irony as a Tool for Judging People

Marvin Mudrick

Marvin Mudrick argues that Elizabeth's irony under-
rides her judgment of others. According to Mudrick,
she first classifies people into one of two categories
—simple or intricate—and then, as an ironic spectator, distinguishes differences among those in each
category. Mudrick concludes that Elizabeth easily
makes correct distinctions in her observations of
simple people, but she is deceived by the intricate
ones and makes mistakes. Marvin Mudrick taught
English at the University of California at Santa Barbara and at Queens College of the City University of
New York. He is the editor of *Conrad: A Collection of
Critical Essays* and the author of *On Culture and Literature* and *The Man and the Machine.*

In *Pride and Prejudice,* for the first time, Jane Austen allows
her heroine to share her own characteristic response to the
world. Elizabeth Bennet tells Darcy:

> Follies and nonsense, whims and inconsistencies do divert
> me, I own, and I laugh at them whenever I can.

The response is not only characteristic of Elizabeth and her
author, but consciously and articulately aimed at by both of
them. Both choose diversion; and both, moreover, look for
their diversion in the people about them. . . .

ELIZABETH CLASSIFIES PEOPLE AND
DISCRIMINATES WITHIN CATEGORIES

"Character" gains a general overtone: with Elizabeth's qual-
ifying adjective, it becomes not only the summation of a
single personality, but the summation of a type, the fixing of
the individual into a category. So Elizabeth sets herself up as
an ironic spectator, able and prepared to judge and classify,

Reprinted from *Jane Austen: Irony as Defense and Discovery,* by Marvin Mudrick.
(Princeton, NJ: Princeton University Press, 1952), by permission of the Estate of Marvin Mudrick.

already making the first large division of the world into two sorts of people: the simple ones, those who give themselves away out of shallowness (as Bingley fears) or perhaps openness (as Elizabeth implies) or an excess of affectation (as Mr. Collins will demonstrate); and the intricate ones, those who cannot be judged and classified so easily, who are "the most amusing" to the ironic spectator because they offer the most formidable challenge to his powers of detection and analysis. Into one of these preliminary categories, Elizabeth fits everybody she observes.

Elizabeth shares her author's characteristic response of comic irony, defining incongruities without drawing them into a moral context; and, still more specifically, Elizabeth's vision of the world as divided between the simple and the intricate is, in *Pride and Prejudice* at any rate, Jane Austen's vision also. This identification between the author and her heroine establishes, in fact, the whole ground pattern of judgment in the novel. The first decision we must make about anyone, so Elizabeth suggests and the author confirms by her shaping commentary, is not moral but psychological, not whether he is good or bad, but whether he is simple or intricate: whether he may be disposed of as fixed and predictable or must be recognized as variable, perhaps torn between contradictory motives, intellectually or emotionally complex, unsusceptible to a quick judgment.

Once having placed the individual in his category, we must proceed to discriminate him from the others there; and, in the category of simplicity at least, Elizabeth judges as accurately as her author. Jane Austen allows the "simple" characters to have no surprises for Elizabeth, and, consequently, none for us. They perform, they amuse; but we never doubt that we know what they are, and why they act as they do. . . .

ELIZABETH JUDGES SIMPLE PEOPLE ACCURATELY

Mr. Collins and Lady Catherine, though "simple," also differ from Lydia and Mrs. Bennet at least to the extent that Elizabeth can observe them more freely, without the sense of shame and responsibility she must feel toward her mother and sister. Mr. Collins is, indeed, so remote from Elizabeth's personal concerns that she and the reader can enjoy him as a pure fool, unweighted by moral import. The fact that he is a clergyman underscores his foolishness and moral nullity:

> I have been so fortunate as to be distinguished by the patronage
> of the Right Honourable Lady Catherine de Bourgh, widow of
> Sir Lewis de Bourgh, whose bounty and beneficence has pre-
> ferred me to the valuable rectory of this parish, where it shall
> be my earnest endeavour to demean myself with grateful re-
> spect towards her Ladyship, and be ever ready to perform those
> rites and ceremonies which are instituted by the Church of En-
> gland. As a clergyman, moreover, I feel it my duty to promote
> and establish the blessing of peace in all families within the
> reach of my influence; and on these grounds I flatter myself
> that my present overtures of good-will are highly commend-
> able, and that the circumstance of my being next in the entail[1]
> of Longbourn estate, will be kindly overlooked on your side,
> and not lead you to reject the offered olive branch.

"'Can he be a sensible man, sir?'" Elizabeth asks; and her
father replies:

> No, my dear; I think not. I have great hopes of finding him
> quite the reverse. There is a mixture of servility and self-
> importance in his letter, which promises well. I am impatient
> to see him.

Mr. Bennet's expectation of amusement is fulfilled many times
over. "Mr. Collins was not a sensible man," as the author begins a superfluous descriptive paragraph; and his fatuity, syco-
phancy, conceit, and resolutely unprejudiced wife-hunting are
given ample range. Wherever he goes, whatever he does, he
remains unshakably foolish. Elizabeth's declining his proposal, once he can believe that it is not to be ascribed to the
"usual practice of elegant females," clouds his jauntiness for a
moment; but he recovers soon enough to propose as fervently
to Charlotte Lucas three days later, and when he leaves Longbourn he wishes his "fair cousins . . . health and happiness, not
excepting my cousin Elizabeth." As he likes to be useful to
Lady Catherine, so he is useful to the plot: he provides a place
for Elizabeth to visit, where she can observe Lady Catherine
and see Darcy again; he draws out his "affable and condescending" patroness for Elizabeth's edification; he serves as a
medium through which Lady Catherine's opinions on events
in the Bennet family are graciously transmitted to the Bennets.
And always he remains firm in the conviction of his importance and dignity, of his place at the center—or a little off the
matriarchal center—of the universe, whether he is almost
walking on air in contemplation of the advantage of Rosings:

> Words were insufficient for the elevation of his feelings; and
> he was obliged to walk about the room, while Elizabeth tried
> to unite civility and truth in a few short sentences.

1. a predetermined order of succession, as to an estate

or warning Elizabeth against a "precipitate closure" with Darcy's suit, or offering his clerical opinion on Lydia and Wickham:

> I must not . . . refrain from declaring my amazement, at hearing that you received the young couple into your house as soon as they were married. It was an encouragement of vice; and had I been the rector of Longbourn, I should very strenuously have opposed it. You ought certainly to forgive them as a christian, but never to admit them in your sight, or allow their names to be mentioned in your hearing.

Like Mr. Collins, Lady Catherine is chiefly amusing because of the incongruity between the importance she assumes to herself and the actual influence she exercises upon the story. At first glance, she is, of course, far more formidable than Mr. Collins:

> Her air was not conciliating, nor was her manner of receiving them, such as to make her visitors forget their inferior rank.

She has her worshipful courtier in Mr. Collins, who, dining at Rosings, "looked as if he felt that life could furnish nothing greater." And she is confident of having her judgments explicitly followed:

> . . . delivering her opinion on every subject in so decisive a manner as proved that she was not used to have her judgement controverted. . . . Elizabeth found that nothing was beneath this great Lady's attention, which could furnish her with an occasion of dictating to others.

Yet, in the story at least, she never does what she thinks she is doing or wishes to do. It is true—as Elizabeth remarks— that "Lady Catherine has been of infinite use, which ought to make her happy, for she loves to be of use." She is useful to the story; but only in ways she is unaware of and would repudiate with outrage if she knew of them. By her insulting condescension toward Elizabeth, she helps Darcy to balance off his distaste of Mrs. Bennet's not dissimilar shortcomings. She provokes Elizabeth into asserting her own independence of spirit, even to the point of impertinence. In her arrogant effort to dissuade Elizabeth from accepting Darcy, she gives Elizabeth the opportunity to set her own proud value upon herself as an individual, and later, having angrily brought the news to Darcy, encourages him to believe that Elizabeth may not refuse him a second time. Lady Catherine is a purely comic figure, not because she is not potentially powerful and dangerous in the authority that

rank and wealth confer upon her, but because she is easily
known for what she is, and because the lovers are in a position—Darcy by his own rank and wealth, Elizabeth by her
spirit and intelligence—to deny her power altogether.

This quality of powerlessness is, indeed, peculiar to Elizabeth's, and the author's, whole category of simplicity: not
merely in Mrs. Bennet, Lydia, Mr. Collins, and Lady Catherine, but in the predictably malicious Miss Bingley, in single-
postured simpletons like Sir William Lucas and Mary Bennet, down to an unrealized function like Georgiana Darcy.
They are powerless, that is, at the center of the story. They
cannot decisively divert Elizabeth's or Darcy's mind and
purpose because they cannot cope with the adult personality that either of the lovers presents. They are powerless, ul-
timately, because they are not themselves adult. They convince us of their existence (except, perhaps, Georgiana and
Mary), sometimes even brilliantly; but they are not sufficiently complex or self-aware to be taken at the highest level
of seriousness. Elizabeth's judgment of them is, then, primarily psychological, not moral: they have not grown to a
personal stature significantly measurable by moral law.
However Elizabeth may console Bingley that a "deep, intricate character" may be no more "estimable than such a one
as yours," the fact is that though she finds simplicity comfortable or amusing, it is only intricacy, complexity of spirit,
that she finds fascinating, deserving of pursuit and capture,
susceptible to a grave moral judgment. . . .

DISTINCTION REQUIRES SELF-AWARENESS; COMPLEXITY DEMANDS DISTINCTIONS

In *Pride and Prejudice*, there is no compulsion—personal,
thematic, or moral—toward denying the heroine her own
powers of judgment. There is, on the contrary, a thematic
need for the heroine to display a subtle, accurate, a perceiv-
ing mind. In *Pride and Prejudice*, as in the previous novels,
Jane Austen deals with the distinction between false moral
values and true; but she is also dealing here with a distinction antecedent to the moral judgment—the distinction between the simple personality, unequipped with that self-
awareness which alone makes choice seem possible, and
the complex personality, whose most crucial complexity is
its awareness, of self and others. This distinction, which in
her youthful defensive posture Jane Austen has tended to

make only between her characters and herself, she here establishes internally, between two categories of personality within the novel. The distinction is, in fact, one that every character in *Pride and Prejudice* must make if he can; and the complex characters—Elizabeth and Darcy among them— justify their complexity by making it, and trying to live by its implications, through all their lapses of arrogance, prejudice, sensuality, and fear. Elizabeth is aware because, in the novel's climate of adult decision, she must be so to survive with our respect and interest.

Yet the distinction must be made in a social setting, by human beings fallible, if for no other reason, because of their own social involvement. The province of *Pride and Prejudice* —as always in Jane Austen's novels—is marriage in an acquisitive[2] society. Elizabeth herself, being young, attractive, and unmarried, is at the center of it. . . .

ELIZABETH DECEIVED BY THE COMPLEX

She can tag and dismiss the blatantly simple persons very well; it is when she moves away from these toward ambiguity and self-concealment, toward persons themselves aware enough to interest and engage her, that her youth and inexperience and emotional partiality begin to deceive her. They deceive her first with Charlotte Lucas. The two girls have been good friends. Charlotte, according to the author, is a "sensible, intelligent young woman," and she shares Elizabeth's taste for raillery and social generalization. Even when Charlotte offers her altogether cynical views on courtship and marriage, Elizabeth refuses to take her at her word:

> "Happiness in marriage is entirely a matter of chance. If the dispositions of the parties are ever so well known to each other, or ever so similar before-hand, it does not advance their felicity in the least. They always continue to grow sufficiently unlike afterwards to have their share of vexation; and it is better to know as little as possible of the defects of the person with whom you are to pass your life."
>
> "You make me laugh, Charlotte; but it is not sound. You know it is not sound, and that you would never act in this way yourself."

It is not that Elizabeth misjudges Charlotte's capabilities, but that she underestimates the strength of the pressures acting upon her. Charlotte is twenty-seven, unmarried, not pretty, not well-to-do, living in a society which treats a penniless old maid

2. characterized by a strong desire to gain and possess

less as a joke than as an exasperating burden upon her family. But Elizabeth is inexperienced enough, at the beginning, to judge in terms of personality only. She recognizes Mr. Collins' total foolishness and Charlotte's intelligence, and would never have dreamed that any pressure could overcome so natural an opposition. Complex and simple, aware and unaware, do not belong together—except that in marriages made by economics they often unite, however obvious the mismatching. . . .

It is the social façade of the complex person that deceives Elizabeth. She can penetrate her father's, out of sympathetic familiarity and concern; but Charlotte's has deceived her. Wickham's takes her in altogether; and by contrast with Wickham's, by the contrast which Wickham himself takes care to emphasize in his own support, Darcy's façade seems disagreeable indeed, or rather a clear window on a dis-agreeable spirit.

Darcy's function as the character most difficult for the heroine to interpret, and yet most necessary for her to inter-pret if *she* is to make a proper decision in the only area of choice her society leaves open, his simultaneous role as the heroine's puzzle and her only possible hero, is clearly marked out during the action. From Elizabeth's point of view, in fact, the process of the interpretation of Darcy's per-sonality from disdain through doubt to admiration is repre-sented with an extraordinarily vivid and convincing minute-ness. Nevertheless, Darcy himself remains unachieved: we recognize his effects upon Elizabeth, without recognizing that he exists independently of them. . . .

The characters, most conspicuously Darcy, must shift for themselves, or, rather, they fall automatically into the grooves prepared for them by hundreds of novels of senti-ment and sensibility.

Only Elizabeth does not. She may yield temporarily to a kind of homeless moralizing on Lydia's disgrace, she may be rather obvious and stiff in acquainting herself with Darcy's virtues at last; but the lapses are minor, and they never seriously dim her luminous vigor, her wit, curiosity, discrimination, and inde-pendence. If the novel does not collapse in the predictabili-ties of the denouement, it is because Elizabeth has from the outset been presented in a depth specific and vital enough to resist flattening, because she remains what she has been— a complex person in search of conclusions about people in society, and on the way to her unique and crucial choice.

ELIZABETH'S IRONY SUSTAINS THE ACTION

She observes, and her shield and instrument together is irony. . . . Elizabeth's third dimension is irony; and it is her irony that fills out and sustains the action. Her slightest perception of incongruity reverberates through the scene, and from it out into the atmosphere of the book. . . . There is, above all, the perpetual exuberant yet directed irony of her conversation, especially as she uses it to sound Darcy. . . .

She never gives up her first principle: to separate the simple personality from the complex, and to concentrate her attention and interest on the latter. Her point of reference is always the complex individual, the individual aware and capable of choice. Her own pride is in her freedom, to observe, to analyze, to choose; her continual mistake is to forget that, even for her, there is only one area of choice—marriage—and that this choice is subject to all the powerful and numbing pressures of an acquisitive society. . . .

In *Pride and Prejudice*, Jane Austen's irony has developed into an instrument of discrimination between the people who are simple reproductions of their social type and the people with individuality and will, between the unaware and the aware. . . . The irony is internal, it does not take disturbing tangents toward the author's need for self-vindication: even self-defensive, it is internal and consistent. . . .

Irony here rejects chiefly to discover and illuminate; and, though its setting is the same stratified, materialistic, and severely regulated society, its new text and discovery—its new character, in fact, whom Jane Austen has hitherto allowed only herself to impersonate—is the free individual.

Irony Reveals Character and Advances the Drama

Reuben Arthur Brower

Reuben Arthur Brower argues that Austen's irony both creates simple and complex characters and advances the story. His first analysis involves Mr. and Mrs. Bennet, whose opening scene reveals them so completely that little interpretation is needed. Brower then analyzes more complex Elizabeth-Darcy scenes in which Austen suggests ironic ambiguity, which in turn heightens the complexity of the characters and the situations at the next stage in the couple's relationship. Brower concludes that only complex characters with adult minds speak with enough ironic ambiguity to require interpretation. Reuben Arthur Brower has taught English at Harvard University. He is the author of *Alexander Pope: The Poetry of Allusion*, *Hero and Saint: Shakespeare and the Graeco-Roman Heroic Tradition*, and *Mirror on Mirror: Translation, Imitation, and Parody.*

Many pages of *Pride and Prejudice* can be read as sheer poetry of wit, as Pope without couplets.[1] The antitheses are almost as frequent and almost as varied; the play of ambiguities is certainly as complex; the orchestration of tones is as precise and subtle. As in the best of Pope, the displays of ironic wit are not without imaginative connection; what looks most diverse is really most similar, and ironies are linked by vibrant reference to basic certainties. There are passages too in which the rhythmical pattern of the sentence approaches the formal balance of the heroic couplet:

1. Eighteenth-century British poet Alexander Pope is famous for his witty rhymed couplets, a form with both grammatical structure and idea complete within itself.

> Mr. Bennet was so odd a mixture of quick parts, sarcastic humour, reserve, and caprice, that the experience of three and twenty years had been insufficient to make his wife understand his character. *Her* mind was less difficult to develope. She was a woman of mean understanding, little information, and uncertain temper. When she was discontented she fancied herself nervous. The business of her life was to get her daughters married; its solace was visiting and news.

The triumph of the novel—whatever its limitations may be— lies in combining such poetry of wit with the dramatic structure of fiction. In historical terms, to combine the traditions of poetic satire with those of the sentimental novel, that was Jane Austen's feat in *Pride and Prejudice*.

For the 'bright and sparkling,' seemingly centrifugal play of irony is dramatically functional. It makes sense as literary art, the sense with which a writer is most concerned. The repartee, while constantly amusing, delineates characters and their changing relations and points the way to a climactic moment in which the change is most clearly recognized. Strictly speaking, this union of wit and drama is achieved with complete success only in the central sequence of *Pride and Prejudice*, in the presentation of Elizabeth's and Darcy's gradual revaluation of each other. . . .

THE BENNETS REVEALED IN PERFECT IRONY

Her blend of ironic wit and drama may be seen in its simplest form in the first chapter of the novel, in the dialogue between Mr. and Mrs. Bennet on the topic of Mr. Bingley's leasing Netherfield Park. Every remark which each makes, Mrs. Bennet petulantly, and Mr. Bennet perversely, bounces off the magnificent opening sentence:

> It is a truth universally acknowledged, that a single man in possession of a good fortune, must be in want of a wife.

The scene that follows dramatizes the alternatives implied in 'universally,' Mrs. Bennet reminding us of one; and Mr. Bennet, of the other:

> 'My dear Mr. Bennet,' said his lady to him one day, 'have you heard that Netherfield Park is let at last?'
>
> Mr. Bennet replied that he had not.
>
> 'But it is,' returned she; 'for Mrs. Long has just been here, and she told me all about it.'
>
> Mr. Bennet made no answer.
>
> 'Do not you want to know who has taken it?' cried his wife impatiently.
>
> '*You* want to tell me, and I have no objection to hearing it.'

This was invitation enough.

'Why, my dear, you must know, Mrs. Long says that Netherfield is taken by a young man of large fortune from the north of England; that he came down on Monday in a chaise and four to see the place, and was so much delighted with it that he agreed with Mr. Morris immediately; that he is to take possession before Michaelmas, and some of his servants are to be in the house by the end of next week.'

'What is his name?'

'Bingley.'

'Is he married or single?'

'Oh! single, my dear, to be sure! A single man of large fortune; four or five thousand a year. What a fine thing for our girls!'

'How so? how can it affect them?'

'My dear Mr. Bennet,' replied his wife, 'how can you be so tiresome! You must know that I am thinking of his marrying one of them.'

'Is that his design in settling here?'

'Design! nonsense, how can you talk so!'

A parallel appears in the opening of Pope's Epistle, 'Of the Characters of Women':

Nothing so true as what you once let fall,
'Most Women have no Characters at all,'

a pronouncement immediately followed by a series of portraits showing that women have 'characters' in one sense if not in another. It is also easy to find counterparts in Pope's satirical mode for Mr. Bennet's extreme politeness of address, his innocent queries, and his epigrammatic turns. The character that emerges from this dialogue is almost that of a professional satirist: Mr. Bennet is a man of quick parts and sarcastic humor, altogether a most unnatural father. Mrs. Bennet speaks another language; *her* talk does not crackle with irony and epigram; *her* sentences run in quite another mold. They either go on too long or break up awkwardly in impulsive exclamations; this is the talk of a person of 'mean understanding' and 'uncertain temper.'

But though the blended art of this scene is admirable, a limitation appears. Mr. and Mrs. Bennet are so perfectly done that little more is left to be expressed. Variety or forward movement in the drama will almost surely be difficult, which obviously proves to be the case. The sequences that depend most closely on the opening scene—those concerned with the business of getting the Bennet daughters married—are all amusingly ironic, but relatively static as drama. As Mrs. Bennet contrives to join Jane and Bingley, to marry one daughter to Mr. Collins, and to further Lydia's exploits with the military, father, mother, and daughters remain in very nearly the same dramatic positions. True enough, the last of these sequences ends in a catastrophe. But the connection between Lydia's downfall and the earlier scenes of ironic comedy in which Mr. and Mrs. Bennet are opposed is not fully expressed. Lydia's behavior 'leads to this,' . . . but Lydia is too scantly presented in relation to her parents or to Wickham to prepare us adequately for her bad end. We accept it if at all as literary convention. Incidentally, we might conjecture that the marriage-market sequences belong to the early version of *Pride and Prejudice*, or at least that they are examples of Jane Austen's earlier manner. . . .

EARLY DARCY-ELIZABETH DIALOGUES DEFINE CHARACTER THROUGH IRONY

In portraying the gradual change in Elizabeth's estimate of Darcy and in his attitude to her, Jane Austen achieves a perfect harmony between the rich ambiguity of ironic dialogue and the movement toward the climactic scenes in which the new estimate is revealed. I shall limit my discussion to scenes from the Elizabeth-Darcy narrative through the episode in which Elizabeth recognizes her 'change in sentiment.' Let us first read Jane Austen's dialogue as poetry of wit, disregarding for the time being any forward movement in the drama, and observing the variety of the irony and the unity of effect achieved through recurrent patterns and through assumptions shared by writer and reader. As in our reading of Pope, we may in this way appreciate the extraordinary richness of ironic texture and the imaginative continuity running through the play of wit. In analyzing the ironies and the assumptions, we shall see how intensely dramatic the dialogue is, dramatic in the sense of defining characters through the way they speak and are spoken about. . . .

Take for example the dialogue in which Sir William Lucas attempts to interest Mr. Darcy in dancing:

> Elizabeth at that instant moving towards them, he was struck with the notion of doing a very gallant thing, and called out to her,
> 'My dear Miss Eliza, why are not you dancing?—Mr. Darcy, you must allow me to present this young lady to you as a very desirable partner.—You cannot refuse to dance, I am sure, when so much beauty is before you.' And taking her hand, he would have given it to Mr. Darcy, who, though extremely surprised, was not

unwilling to receive it, when she instantly drew back, and said with some discomposure to Sir William,

'Indeed, Sir, I have not the least intention of dancing.—I entreat you not to suppose that I moved this way in order to beg for a partner.'

Mr. Darcy with grave propriety requested to be allowed the honour of her hand; but in vain. Elizabeth was determined; nor did Sir William at all shake her purpose by his attempt at persuasion.

'You excel so much in the dance, Miss Eliza, that it is cruel to deny me the happiness of seeing you; and though this gentleman dislikes the amusement in general, he can have no objection, I am sure, to oblige us for one half hour.'

'Mr. Darcy is all politeness,' said Elizabeth, smiling.

'He is indeed—but considering the inducement, my dear Miss Eliza, we cannot wonder at his complaisance; for who would object to such a partner?'

Elizabeth looked archly,[2] and turned away.

'Mr. Darcy is all politeness': the statement, as Elizabeth might say, has a 'teazing' variety of meanings. Mr. Darcy is polite in the sense indicated by 'grave propriety,' that is, he shows the courtesy appropriate to a gentleman—which is the immediate, public meaning of Elizabeth's compliment. But 'grave propriety,' being a very limited form of politeness, reminds us forcibly of Mr. Darcy's earlier behavior. His 'gravity' at the ball had been 'forbidding and disagreeable.' 'Grave propriety' may also mean the bare civility of 'the proudest, most disagreeable man in the world.' So Elizabeth's compliment has an ironic twist: she smiles and looks 'archly.' 'All politeness' has also quite another meaning. Mr. Darcy 'was not unwilling to receive' her hand. He is polite in more than the public proper sense; his gesture shows that he is interested in Elizabeth as a person. Her archness and her smile have for the reader an added ironic value: Elizabeth's interpretation of Darcy's manner may be quite wrong. Finally, there is the embracing broadly comic irony of Sir William's action. 'Struck with the notion of doing a very gallant thing,' he is pleasantly unconscious of what he is in fact doing and of what Elizabeth's remark may mean to her and to Darcy.

LATER DARCY-ELIZABETH DIALOGUES SUGGEST LAYERS OF IRONIC MEANING

A similar cluster of possibilities appears in another conversation in which Darcy asks Elizabeth to dance with him:

2. mischievously

. . . soon afterwards Mr. Darcy, drawing near Elizabeth, said to her—

'Do not you feel a great inclination, Miss Bennet, to seize such an opportunity of dancing a reel?'

She smiled, but made no answer. He repeated the question, with some surprise at her silence.

'Oh!' said she, 'I heard you before; but I could not immediately determine what to say in reply. You wanted me, I know, to say "Yes," that you might have the pleasure of despising my taste; but I always delight in overthrowing those kind of schemes, and cheating a person of their premeditated contempt. I have therefore made up my mind to tell you, that I do not want to dance a reel at all—and now despise me if you dare.'

'Indeed I do not dare.'

Elizabeth, having rather expected to affront him, was amazed at his gallantry; but there was a mixture of sweetness and archness in her manner which made it difficult for her to affront anybody; and Darcy had never been so bewitched by any woman as he was by her. He really believed, that were it not for the inferiority of her connections, he should be in some danger.

Miss Bingley saw, or suspected enough to be jealous; and her great anxiety for the recovery of her dear friend Jane, received some assistance from her desire of getting rid of Elizabeth.

She often tried to provoke Darcy into disliking her guest, by talking of their supposed marriage, and planning his happiness in such an alliance.

Again Mr. Darcy's request may be interpreted more or less pleasantly, depending on whether we connect it with his present or past behavior. Again Elizabeth's attack on Darcy and her archness have an irony beyond the irony intended by the speaker. But the amusement of this dialogue lies especially in the variety of possible tones which we detect in Darcy's speeches. Elizabeth hears his question as expressing 'premeditated contempt' and scorn of her own taste. But from Mr. Darcy's next remark and the comment which follows, and from his repeating his question and showing 'some surprise,' we may hear in his request a tone expressive of some interest, perhaps only gallantry, perhaps, as Elizabeth later puts it 'somewhat of a friendlier nature.' We could take his 'Indeed I do not dare' as pure gallantry (Elizabeth's version) or as a sign of conventional 'marriage intentions' (Miss Bingley's interpretation), if it were not for the nice reservation, 'He really believed, that were it not for the inferiority of her connections, he should be in some danger.'

We must hear the remark as spoken with this qualification. This simultaneity of tonal layers can be matched only in the satire of Pope, where, as we have seen, the reader feels the impossibility of adjusting his voice to the rapid changes in tone and the difficulty of representing by a single sound the several sounds he hears as equally appropriate and necessary. Analysis such as I have been making shows clearly how arbitrary and how thin any stage rendering of *Pride and Prejudice* must be. No speaking voice could possibly represent the variety of tones conveyed to the reader by such interplay of dialogue and comment.

It would be easy enough to produce more of these dialogues, especially on the subject of music or dancing, each with its range of crisply differentiated meanings. Similar patterns of irony recur many times. Mr. Darcy makes his inquiries (polite or impolite), asking with a smile (scornful or encouraging) questions that may be interpreted as pompous and condescending or gallant and well-disposed. So Mr. Darcy cross-examines Elizabeth in the scene in which their 'superior dancing' gives such pleasure to Sir William:

'What think you of books?' said he, smiling.

'Books—Oh! no.—I am sure we never read the same, or not with the same feelings.'

'I am sorry you think so; but if that be the case, there can at least be no want of subject.—We may compare our different opinions.'

'No—I cannot talk of books in a ball-room; my head is always full of something else.'

'The *present* always occupies you in such scenes—does it?' said he, with a look of doubt.

When connected with a hint of Darcy's changing attitude, that 'look of doubt,' Elizabeth's arch comments take on the added ironic value we have noted in other conversations.

Earlier in this dialogue, Darcy and Elizabeth run through the same sort of question and answer gamut, and with very nearly the same ironic dissonances:

He smiled, and assured her that whatever she wished him to say should be said.

'Very well.—That reply will do for the present.—Perhaps by and bye I may observe that private balls are much pleasanter than public ones.—But *now* we may be silent.'

'Do you talk by rule then, while you are dancing?'

'Sometimes. One must speak a little, you know. It would look odd to be entirely silent for half an hour together, and yet for the advantage of *some*, conversation ought to be so arranged as that they may have the trouble of saying as little as possible.'

'Are you consulting your own feelings in the present case, or do you imagine that you are gratifying mine?'

'Both,' replied Elizabeth archly; 'for I have always seen a great similarity in the turn of our minds.—We are each of an unsocial, taciturn disposition, unwilling to speak, unless we expect to say something that will amaze the whole room, and be handed down to posterity with all the eclat[3] of a proverb.'

'This is no very striking resemblance of your own character, I am sure,' said he.

When Darcy himself is being quizzed he frequently remarks on his own behavior in a way that may be sublimely smug or simply self-respecting, as for example in his comment on his behavior at the first of the Hertfordshire balls:

'I certainly have not the talent which some people possess,' said Darcy, 'of conversing easily with those I have never seen before. I cannot catch their tone of conversation, or appear interested in their concerns, as I often see done.'

But these conversations are not simply sets of ironic meanings; they are in more than a trivial sense *jeux d'esprit,* the play of an adult mind. (The sophistication they imply is of a kind which, as [critic] John Jay Chapman once remarked, is Greek and French, rather than English.) The fun in Jane Austen's dialogue has a serious point; or rather, the fun is the point. The small talk is the focus for her keen sense of the variability of character, for her awareness of the possibility that the same remark or action has very different meanings in different relations. What most satisfies us in reading the dialogue in *Pride and Prejudice* is Jane Austen's awareness that it is difficult to know any complex person, that knowledge of a man like Darcy is an interpretation and a construction, not a simple absolute. . . .

ONLY THE COMPLEX CHARACTERS WITH ADULT MINDS REQUIRE INTERPRETATION

But it is only the complex persons, the 'intricate characters,' that require and merit interpretation, as Elizabeth points out in the pleasant conversation in which she tells Bingley that she 'understands him perfectly':

'You begin to comprehend me, do you?' cried he, turning towards her.

'Oh! yes,—I understand you perfectly.'

3. great brilliance

'I wish I might take this for a compliment; but to be so easily seen through I am afraid is pitiful.'

'That is as it happens. It does not necessarily follow that a deep, intricate character is more or less estimable than such a one as yours.'

'Lizzy,' cried her mother, 'remember where you are, and do not run on in the wild manner that you are suffered to do at home.'

'I did not know before,' continued Bingley immediately, 'that you were a studier of character. It must be an amusing study.'

'Yes; but intricate characters are the *most* amusing. They have at least that advantage.'

'The country,' said Darcy, 'can in general supply but few subjects for such a study. In a country neighbourhood you move in a very confined and unvarying society.'

'But people themselves alter so much, that there is something new to be observed in them for ever.'

Elizabeth's remark with its ironic application to Darcy indicates the interest that makes the book 'go' and shows the type of awareness we are analyzing. 'Intricate characters are the *most* amusing,' because their behavior can be taken in so many ways, because they are not always the same people. The man we know today is a different man tomorrow. Naturally, we infer, people will not be equally puzzling to every judge. Mr. Bingley and Jane find Mr. Darcy a much less 'teazing' man than Elizabeth does. It is only the Elizabeths, the adult minds, who will observe something new in the 'same' people.

Such are the main assumptions behind the irony of *Pride and Prejudice*, as they are expressed through conversational studies of Darcy's character. In marked contrast with the opening scene of the novel, there is in these dialogues no nondramatic statement of the ironist's position, a further sign that in shaping the Elizabeth-Darcy sequence Jane Austen was moving away from the modes of satire toward more purely dramatic techniques.

Wit Embedded Within Dialogue

Jan Fergus

Jan Fergus argues that Austen's wit, both in and out of
dialogue, exposes misperceptions and incongruities.
Fergus identifies four particular uses of wit. Mr. Bennet's wit—expressed more through narrative than dialogue—reveals his disdain for his wife. Wit embedded
in dialogue exposes characters' general faults and
foibles, giving the reader immediate pleasure. The effects of wit expressed in ironic plot turns are delayed
until the reader gains new information or recognizes
the significance of already available information. Finally, Austen's high comedy exposes the characters'
unstated motives beneath their polite, clever public
personas. Jan Fergus is assistant professor at Lehigh
University and has taught at Brooklyn College of the
City University of New York. She has written about
Jane Austen and morality in literature.

The best effects in *Pride and Prejudice* are achieved because
Austen experiments with and masters other elements in the
comedy of manners: wit and dialogue. The two are distinct,
though sometimes confused. Dialogue may or may not be
witty, while wit need not form part of anything deserving the
name of dialogue, which implies reciprocity: at least in
some sense, ideas and opinions are being exchanged among
reasonably attentive speakers, not merely displayed by
them.

Whether wit appears in dialogue, so understood, or not,
an author can count on favourable responses to it and to
characters responsible for it, since pleasure in well-phrased
judgments or criticisms, and in perceptions or exposures of
incongruity, is essentially an intellectual rather than a moral
response. If wit is to be registered as anything but delightful,

extremely skilful treatment is needed. . . . In *Pride and Prejudice*, [Austen's] demands on the reader's emotions in response to wit are less complex and less strenuous, for her interest lies primarily in a more easily-handled theme. She exposes the imperception rather than the ugliness which pleasure in wit can produce. Nevertheless, she does demand that the reader register the inaccuracies of judgment encouraged by Elizabeth's wit. In her treatment of Mr Bennet, she requires a yet more complex response.

MR BENNET'S WIT APPEARS IN NARRATIVE, NOT DIALOGUE

In Chapter II, Mr Bennet's wit displays his contempt for his wife and provokes her to expose herself before their children. Austen inserts this scene as a possible check to the reader's simple delight in Elizabeth's wit even before that delight can occur, for Elizabeth says nothing remarkable until Chapter IV. Although Chapter II is composed almost entirely of speeches, they do not constitute real dialogue. Mr and Mrs Bennet talk at cross-purposes. Mrs Bennet is wholly oblivious to her husband's mockery, but neither her idiocy nor her blindness can excuse him. Mr Bennet's wit seldom appears in dialogue whatever his company, for his ironic detachment usually precludes it. At the Netherfield ball, for example, he puts a stop to Mary's indifferent singing with an isolated remark, 'That will do extremely well, child. You have delighted us long enough. Let the other young ladies have time to exhibit'. When Elizabeth tries to persuade him to prevent Lydia's going to Brighton, he replies, 'Lydia will never be easy till she has exposed herself in some public place or other, and we can never expect her to do it with so little expense or inconvenience to her family as under the present circumstances'. This remark is as irresponsible as it is amusing. It is also firmly attached to the plot, for in Brighton Lydia does expose herself: she elopes with Wickham, an action that brings about the dénouement. The rest of the scene between Elizabeth and her father counterpoints her earnestness with his irresponsibility. Although in speaking to Elizabeth Mr Bennet can be serious, even affectionate, his detachment and withdrawal usually operate even then. His only 'dialogue' occurs at the end, when he appeals to Elizabeth to reconsider her engagement. Moved as he is in the scene, he quickly resumes his ironic stance once assured that Elizabeth loves Darcy.

WIT EMBEDDED IN DIALOGUE

Wit is, fortunately, more a part of dialogue in *Pride and Prejudice* than separable from it. . . . And the wit which [Austen] embeds in dialogue is at least as immediately delightful as Mr Bennet's and has far more complex uses in controlling the reader's response to the characters. The popular judgment that dialogue is the great achievement of *Pride and Prejudice* is certainly correct, although admiration is usually confined to its wit and its success in revealing character. Besides its entertaining and dramatic qualities, however, the witty dialogue among groups of characters in *Pride and Prejudice* gives fuller expression to feeling, perception and judgment, and consequently to the themes, than the dialogue of *Sense and Sensibility* and *Northanger Abbey* permits or intends. Without relinquishing earlier techniques of dialogue, Austen experiments with a number of new ones which allow increased expressiveness and which demand increasingly complex responses from readers. . . .

One form of dialogue visible in *Pride and Prejudice* and *Sense and Sensibility* but eliminated later is a legacy from the eighteenth-century novel and supplies social comedy narrowly defined. A number of speakers expose their characteristic faults or foibles by their various responses to a particular event or topic. This form is very common in *Pride and Prejudice.* Chapter V, containing the five-way debate on pride, is a typical example. Some critics cite scenes like this one as evidence that Austen adopts a kind of relativism, but 'relativistic impressionism' is hardly her aim. For her, and for the eighteenth century in general, human motives are fathomable, however complex; human judgments are corrigible, however prone to error; and human misconduct can be understood as folly and vice, not as their modern counterparts, neurosis and a secularized notion of original sin. Austen inherits a comic tradition which assumes that a complete, instructive and morally useful picture of society can be obtained by bringing together characters who exhibit manners, follies and affectations carefully chosen to contrast with each other as much as possible. . . .

The form has undeniable virtues. It allows fools like Mrs Bennet to expose their folly with wonderful economy, while wits like Elizabeth shine by comparison. It can even be used if the follies of rational characters are to be displayed, as in

Sense and Sensibility when Marianne's amusing notion that Colonel Brandon at thirty-five is too old and infirm to love is contrasted with the more accurate views of Mrs Dashwood and Elinor. But the broad, glaring contrasts essential to this form of dialogue disqualify it for the finer discriminations among feelings, perceptions and judgments which are Austen's major interest and which the new techniques of *Pride and Prejudice* accommodate.

Austen's New Techniques Make Finer Discriminations

These new techniques may be divided into two classes according to the effects they produce on the reader. First, effects may be immediate, and will depend on what the reader knows that the characters do not. Or effects may be delayed, and will depend on what the reader either can know but for various reasons does not realize (e.g., that Wickham's account of Darcy is fake), or what he simply cannot know until a later point in the novel or until a second reading. A good example of this last class is linear irony which does not stem directly from Elizabeth's misunderstanding of Darcy and Wickham: Elizabeth's shock at Charlotte's engagement set against Jane's later shock at Elizabeth's. . . .

Austen's ability to make dialogue serve her themes is not confined to the delayed effects supplied by linear irony or by such *tours de force*[1] as Wickham's first conversations with Elizabeth. Most of the dialogue in *Pride and Prejudice* creates immediate effects, either those comic effects typical of eighteenth-century social comedy, or more complex ones which depend on what the reader knows that the characters do not. These complex effects are both emotional and comic. They increase in power the more the reader 'knows'—the more attention he pays—and are Austen's signature and her triumph. The reader has every incentive to read closely, for the more he is aware of the characters' motives, reactions, and misconceptions, the funnier the comedy. . . .

Techniques of Austen's Higher Comedy

When Austen writes mere social comedy, like that of Chapter V, character is necessarily simplified, for the effect depends on broad contrasts; characters merely personify different manners and attitudes. Such comedy is too lucid.

1. a feat requiring great virtuosity

When Austen writes her own higher comedy in *Pride and Prejudice*, she succeeds in permitting characters to expose, beneath the surface restraints of polite, clever talk, their unstated and incongruous (or clashing) motives, judgments and feelings. The range of comic and emotional incongruity which Austen learns to make her dialogue convey and her readers perceive in *Pride and Prejudice* is nicely illustrated, on the one hand, by the early scenes at Netherfield and, on the other, by Darcy's first proposal to Elizabeth. . . .

When Darcy and Elizabeth identify each other's faults of character, the scene is principally comic, for each complacently misunderstands the other's meaning and motives, and the reader knows more than either can. Such comedy is central to the themes and plot of the novel, for Darcy's fault is 'a propensity to hate every body' and Elizabeth's 'wilfully to misunderstand them'. Yet the scene has undercurrents of sexual antagonism and attraction not entirely contained by the comedy of misjudgment enacted on the surface or by the linear irony which allows Elizabeth's and Darcy's judgments of each other to be felt again and again throughout the novel.

This form of dialogue, the source of what may be called Austen's high comedy, is perfectly illustrated by the scene which takes up the first half of Chapter X. The dialogue opens comically, develops emotional undertones and thematic implications through a variety of new techniques, and ends with a higher, more complex comedy than anything promised by its beginning. Austen prefaces this scene by noting that Darcy is writing to his sister, Miss Bingley is praising his efforts, and Elizabeth is 'sufficiently amused' by their 'curious dialogue, . . . exactly in unison with her opinion of each'. The reader should allow this observation to guide his understanding of the entire scene. He should notice that nothing Darcy says shakes Elizabeth's opinion of his pride, conceit and ill temper. The dialogue is so skilfully contrived, however, that while a prejudiced mind, like Elizabeth's, can see these qualities in Darcy's remarks, an open mind will not. When Darcy replies to Miss Bingley's inane question, 'do you always write such charming long letters', with 'They are generally long; but whether always charming, it is not for me to determine', a reader can take its politely repelling irony as evidence that Darcy, neither seeking nor liking Miss Bingley's flattery, puts up with it and her remarkably well. The reader, of course, is better able than Elizabeth to interpret Darcy's behaviour correctly, having information she has not: that Darcy is attracted to Elizabeth and is as well-acquainted with Miss Bingley's jealousy as with her designs on him. These emotions have been amply demonstrated by Darcy's earlier pointed (but still polite) rebuke to Miss Bingley's catty remarks about Elizabeth: 'there is meanness in *all* the arts which ladies sometimes condescend to employ for captivation. Whatever bears affinity to cunning is despicable'. Yet ambiguity is not entirely dispelled by such speeches. A reader can take Darcy's remarks here and in Chapter X as Elizabeth would: evidence of ill-mannered conceit. His appreciation of the finer comedy in these scenes is simply delayed, and the immediate effect for him is purely comic. But it ought to be more complex. The reader should be able to see Darcy as politely, forbearingly ironic in his reception of Miss Bingley's officious compliments and should be aware that Elizabeth is viewing the same behaviour as evidence of his rudeness and his pride. Thus, the reader is asked to respond at several levels. . . . As the scene in Chapter X progresses, its demands on the reader increase. . . .

Extended analysis makes this scene appear more solemn than it is. Austen's touch is light and sure, allowing comic incongruity to modulate brilliantly into a complex clash of wills, judgments and feelings, closing in symmetry but not harmony, each character certain he understands what has passed and confirmed in his original opinion of the others despite all counter-evidence offered within this 'curious dialogue'. The counter-evidence is twofold: Elizabeth, Bingley and Darcy reveal their own characters while they discuss Bingley's, Darcy's and character in general. Discussion of character becomes a common topic in *Pride and Prejudice*, and frequently the character is present, as in this instance, to bear a part in the debate. In Chapter X, all three debaters observe the drama as well as participate in it, so that they are judging and responding to each other's characters, just as the reader must. As a result, the reader is asked to be aware of a threefold process of judgment when he reads the dialogue. On the surface the characters are openly judging Bingley's character. Tacitly, they are judging each other. And finally, the reader is judging them. As one critic says of *Emma*, 'the process of reading runs parallel to the life read about'. This process is only intensified when Darcy and Elizabeth discuss Darcy's character, pretending that Bingley's character is their subject. The reader must also register all the other elements in the dialogue: play of wit; talk on other important issues (character in general, persuasion, humility, pride); and comic and emotional incongruity acted out on qualities other than judgment (Miss Bingley's interest in Darcy, Darcy's and Bingley's friendship, Elizabeth's hostility to it). The technique of linear irony, variously implemented, requires further that the reader recall and re-estimate the scene at various points later in the novel. These requirements alone are quite sufficiently exacting. Added to them is the complex awareness of three processes of judgment, required by Austen's discovery that the characters can talk about judgment while enacting it.

The differences between a scene like this and one in which the topic of conversation is less charged, however thematic it may be, cannot be overemphasized. The debate on pride in Chapter V is apposite.[2] In *Pride and Prejudice,* Austen can be seen in the process of discovering the technique of dialogue she exploits so successfully afterward, the technique of choosing topics for conversation which do not simply reveal differences among characters but which voice, dramatize and complicate the problems of judgment and sympathy which are the themes of the novels. This technique creates cumulative comic and emotional effects. Linear irony does permit these effects to be felt cumulatively in *Pride and Prejudice,* but in *Emma* and *Mansfield Park,* every speech and incident reflects back and forth upon every other. A web is created, not merely a line.

2. strikingly appropriate and relevant

CHRONOLOGY

1770

Romantic poet William Wordsworth born

1772

Romantic poet Samuel Taylor Coleridge born

1773

Boston Tea Party in America, a revolt against British taxation without representation

1775

American War for Independence begins; George Washington in command of American army; Jane Austen born at Steventon, December 16

1776

Thomas Jefferson writes the *Declaration of Independence*, July 4; American political philosopher Thomas Paine publishes *Common Sense*

1778

Fanny Burney publishes *Evelina*

1780

Samuel Johnson, author admired by Austen, publishes *Lives of Poets*

1781

British surrender to Americans in War for Independence

1783

Austen and sister, Cassandra, sent to Mrs. Cawley's school; George Crabbe, Austen's favorite poet, publishes *The Village;* American writer Washington Irving born; Treaty of Paris ends American War for Independence

1785

Austen and Cassandra sent to Abbey School at Reading

1786

Scottish poet Robert Burns publishes *Poems*

1787

Constitutional Convention meets in Philadelphia

1788

Romantic poet Lord Byron born

1789

French Revolution begins with the storming of the Bastille; British poet William Blake publishes *Songs of Innocence;* George Washington becomes first American president; American novelist James Fenimore Cooper born

1791

Austen writes *The History of England,* Cassandra illustrates; Washington, D.C., established as U.S. capital; Bill of Rights adopted

1792

Thomas Paine publishes *The Rights of Man*; Romantic poet Percy Bysshe Shelley born

1793

England goes to war with France; Eli Whitney invents the cotton gin

1794

The Comte de Fuillide, husband of Austen's cousin, guillotined in France

1795

Austen writes first draft of *Elinor and Marianne;* Cassandra engaged to Thomas Fowle; Austen has flirtation with Tomas Lefroy; Romantic poet John Keats born

1796

Austen begins writing *First Impressions* (later retitled *Pride and Prejudice*); Austen's surviving correspondence begins; John Adams elected second American president

1797

Cassandra's fiance dies in the West Indies; Austen finishes *First Impressions,* rejected by Cadell; Austen begins *Sense and Sensibility*; *Susan* written

1798

Wordsworth and Coleridge publish *Lyrical Ballads* with Preface, beginning the Romantic period

1800

Napoleon defeats Austrians; Thomas Jefferson elected third American president; Library of Congress founded

1801

Austen's father retires and moves family to Bath; Austen meets man she expects to marry, but he dies

1802

Harris Bigg-Wither proposes to Austen: she accepts and then breaks engagement; Peace of Ameins with France; American essayist and poet Ralph Waldo Emerson born

1803

Susan sold to Crosby, who does not publish it; war with France resumes; United States buys Louisiana Territory from France for $15 million

1804

Austen begins *The Watsons;* Napoleon becomes emperor of France; American novelist and short story writer Nathaniel Hawthorne born

1804–1816

Lewis and Clark expedition explores American west

1805

Austen's father dies; Austen recasts *Lady Susan,* an epistolary novel written before 1793; Battle of Trafalgar establishes England as supreme naval power

1806

Austen moves to Southampton with mother, Cassandra, and Martha Lloyd; lives with brother Frank and his wife Mary; Noah Webster publishes *Dictionary of the English Language*

1807

Abolition of slave trade in Britain; Wordsworth publishes *Poems*

1808

Napoleon captures Madrid; American Congress stops importation of slaves

1809

Austen moves to Chawton with mother, Cassandra, and Martha Lloyd; American short story writer Edgar Allen Poe born; Abraham Lincoln born; Washington Irving publishes *Knickerbocker's History of New York*

1810

Scottish Romantic novelist Sir Walter Scott publishes *Lady of the Lake*

1811

Austen begins *Mansfield Park; Sense and Sensibility* published

1812

War of 1812 begins between United States and England; British novelist Charles Dickens born; Napoleon's Russian campaign ends with retreat from Moscow; American Academy of Natural Science founded; James Madison elected fourth American president

1813

Pride and Prejudice published; *Mansfield Park* finished

1814

Austen begins *Emma; Mansfield Park* published; Scott publishes *Waverly*, beginning trend of historical novels; British troops burn Washington, D.C.; Francis Scott Key writes "The Star Spangled Banner"

1815

Austen begins *Persuasion;* prince regent "invites" Austen to dedicate *Emma* to him; *Emma* finished and published; *Susan* bought back from Crosby; Napoleon defeated in Battle of Waterloo; Peace of Vienna; peace with America following War of 1812

1816

Austen's health begins to fail; Scott reviews Austen in *Quarterly Review; Persuasion* finished; "Plan of a Novel," finished; James Monroe elected fifth American president

1817

Austen begins *Sandition,* but too ill to finish it; moves to Winchester for better medical care, but dies of Addison's disease on July 18; American essayist Henry David Thoreau born

1818

Persuasion and *Northanger Abbey* published; Scott publishes *Heart of Midlothian;* Mary Shelley publishes *Frankenstein*

1819

Queen Victoria born; American novelist Herman Melville born

FOR FURTHER RESEARCH

ABOUT JANE AUSTEN AND HER WORKS

Walter Allen, *The English Novel: A Short Critical History.* New York: E.P. Dutton, 1954.

Jane Austen, *Pride and Prejudice: An Authoritative Text Backgrounds Reviews and Essays in Criticism.* Ed. Donald J. Gray. New York: W.W. Norton, 1966.

J. D. Austen-Leigh, *A Memoir of Jane Austen,* 1870. In *Persuasion* by Jane Austen, ed. by E. W. Harding. London: Penguin Books, 1965.

Albert C. Baugh, *A Literary History of England.* New York: Appleton-Century-Crofts, 1948.

Julia Prewitt Brown, *Jane Austen's Novels: Social Change and Literary Form.* Cambridge, MA: Harvard University Press, 1979.

Douglas Bush, *Jane Austen.* Masters of World Literature Series, ed. Louis Kronenberger. New York: Macmillan, 1975.

David Cecil, *A Portrait of Jane Austen.* New York: Hill and Wang, 1978.

R.W. Chapman, *Jane Austen: Fact and Problems: The Clark Lectures.* Oxford: Clarendon Press, 1948.

Robert Alan Donovan, *The Shaping Vision: Imagination in the English Novel from Defoe to Dickens.* Ithaca, NY: Cornell University Press, 1966.

Christopher Gillie, *A Preface to Jane Austen.* London: Longman Group, 1974.

John Halperin, *The Life of Jane Austen.* Baltimore, MD: Johns Hopkins University Press, 1984.

Michael Hardwick, *A Guide to Jane Austen.* New York: Charles Scribner's Sons, 1973.

Park Honan, *Jane Austen: Her Life.* New York: St. Martin's Press, 1987.

Elizabeth Jenkins, *Jane Austen.* New York: Grosset & Dunlap, 1949.

R. Brimley Johnson, *Jane Austen.* London: Sheed & Ward, 1927.

Margaret Kennedy, *Jane Austen.* London: Arthur Barker, 1950.

Marghanita Laski, *Jane Austen and Her World.* London: Thames and Hudson, 1969.

Juliet McMaster, *Jane Austen's Achievements: Papers Delivered at the Jane Austen Bicentennial Conference at the University of Alberta.* New York: Barnes and Noble, 1976.

Judith O'Neill, *Critics on Jane Austen: Readings in Literary Criticism.* Coral Gables, FL: University of Miami Press, 1970.

William Lyon Phelps, *The Advance of the English Novel.* New York: Dodd, Mead, 1916.

Joan Rees, *Jane Austen: Woman and Writer.* New York: St. Martin's Press, 1976.

Annette T. Rubinstein, *The Great Tradition in English Literature from Shakespeare to Shaw.* New York: Citadel Press, 1953.

LeRoy W. Smith, *Jane Austen and the Drama of Women.* New York: St. Martin's Press, 1983.

Stuart M. Tave, *Some Words of Jane Austen.* Chicago: University of Chicago Press, 1973.

Ian Watt, ed., *Jane Austen: A Collection of Critical Essays.* Englewood Cliffs, NJ: Prentice-Hall, 1963.

Merryn Williams, *Women in the English Novel, 1800–1900.* New York: St. Martin's Press, 1984.

ABOUT THE TIMES

Asa Briggs, *The Age of Improvement: 1783–1867.* New York: David McKay, 1959.

Will Durant and Ariel Durant, "Johnson's England: 1756–89." In *Rousseau and Revolution,* vol. 10 of *The Story of Civilization.* New York: Simon and Schuster, 1967.

Howard Mumford Jones, *Revolution and Romanticism.* Cambridge, MA: Harvard University Press, 1974.

Dorothy Marshall, *English People in the Eighteenth Century.* London: Longmans, Green, 1956.

J.A. Mazzeo, ed., *Reason and the Imagination: Studies in the History of Ideas 1600–1800.* New York: Columbia University Press, 1962.

J.H. Plumb, *Studies in Social History: A Tribute to G.M. Trevelyan.* London: Longmans, Green, 1955.

Marjorie Quennell and C.H.B. Quennell, *A History of Everyday*

Things in England, vol. 2 1500–1799, vol. 3 1733–1851. London: B.T. Balsford, 1919.

Alfred Leslie Rowse, *The West in English History.* London: Hadder and Stoughton, 1949.

George Macaulay Trevelyan,ʾ*British History in the Nineteenth Century (1782–1901).* New York: Longmans, Green, 1924.

———, *English Social History: A Survey of Six Centuries: Chaucer to Queen Victoria.* London: Longmans, Green, 1943.

———, *History of England.* London: Longmans, Green, 1929.

Earl R. Wasserman, ed., *Aspects of the Eighteenth Century.* Baltimore, MD: Johns Hopkins University Press, 1965.

Basil Willey, *The Eighteenth Century Background: Studies on the Idea of Nature in the Thought of the Period.* New York: Columbia University Press, 1940.

ORGANIZATIONS TO CONTACT

The Jane Austen societies have information or publications available for interested readers. The descriptions are derived from materials provided by the societies themselves. This list was compiled upon the date of publication. Names and phone numbers are subject to change.

The Jane Austen Society
Mr. Tom Carpenter, TD
Jane Austen's House, Chawton
Alton GU34 1SD
U.K.
Tel & Fax 01420 83262
Founded in 1940, the society raised funds to preserve Jane Austen's Cottage in Chawton and turn it into a museum. Besides helping to maintain the museum, the society promotes interest in Jane Austen's life and works. It publishes an annual report of its General Meeting, which includes the address given by the invited speaker, historical notes and articles, and a bibliography of articles and book reviews published the previous year. Lists of available publications and souvenirs can be obtained from the Chawton House address. Copies of the collected annual reports of the society, videos, cassettes, and all books in print relating to Jane Austen may be obtained from

P. & G. Wells Ltd
11 College Street

Winchester
Hampshire S023 9 LX,
U.K.

Jane Austen Society of North America
207 Pinecroft Drive
Raleigh, NC 27609-5232

Founded in 1979, the JASNA brings scholars and enthusiasts together to study and celebrate the genius of Jane Austen. It sponsors an annual conference held in various parts of the United States and supports the forty-seven regional groups. The JASNA publishes a literary journal, *Persuasion,* each December 16, Austen's birthday. It contains reports and papers from the annual conference, articles written by members on Austen, her family, her art, or her times. In addition, the JASNA publishes *Persuasions: Occasional Papers* at irregular intervals and the *JASNA News,* a semiannual newsletter. Membership information is available by contacting

Barbara Larkin
2907 Northland Drive
Columbia, MO 65202
Phone: (314) 474-9682

WORKS BY JANE AUSTEN

Sense and Sensibility First written in 1795 as a series of letters entitled *Elinor and Marianne;* recast as a narrative in 1797 and retitled *Sense and Sensibility* (1811)

Pride and Prejudice First written in 1796, entitled *First Impressions* (1813)

Mansfield Park (1814)

Emma (1815)

Northanger Abbey First written in 1797 and sold but not published as *Susan;* revised in 1816 (1818)

Persuasion (1818)

Lady Susan First written in 1793 or 1794; revised in 1804 (1870)

The Watsons A fragment written in Bath, probably 1805 (1870)

Sandition A fragment written in 1817 (1917)

Letters The standard collection, ed. by R.W. Chapman (1932)

The Works of Jane Austen, ed. R.W. Chapman, vol. VI, *Minor Works,* including "Plan of a Novel" (1954)

INDEX